morning, noon and night

spalding gray

morning, noon and night

farrar, straus and giroux • new york

Farrar, Straus and Giroux
19 Union Square West, New York 10003

Distributed in Canada by Douglas and McIntyre Ltd.
Printed in the United States of America
Designed by Abby Kagan
First edition, 1999

Lyric to Truckin' by Robert Hunter
copyright Ice Nine Publishing Company. Used by permission

Library of Congress Cataloging-in-Publication Data
Gray, Spalding, 1941–
    Morning, noon and night / Spalding Gray. — 1st ed.
        p.   cm.
    ISBN 0-374-29985-4 (alk. paper)
    I. Title.
PS3557.R333M67   1999
812'.54—dc21   99-25630

to kathie
and my parents

We shall not cease from exploration

And the end of all our exploring

Will be to arrive where we started

And know the place for the first time.

Four Quartets

T. S. Eliot

morning, noon and night

I wake and look out the window, scanning the historic cemetery across the street. My eye stops at the old Whalers' Church, where I see the first of the sun's rose-colored light build up behind it and seep out at the edges. This beautiful church was built in 1844 and had an incredible one-hundred-and-sixty-five-foot steeple that the whalers could see in the distance as they rounded Montauk Point. The steeple guided them home after two or three years at sea.

But in 1938 the steeple was blown down by a hurricane and now the church looks like what it is, a perfect example of colonial–Egyptian revival. I mean, it looks like a white clapboard Egyptian tomb, as if George Washington and King Tut could be buried there side by side.

From the old Whalers' Church my eye scans back across the cemetery and goes to Theo, my nine-month-old infant son sleeping beside me. Beside him, I see

Kathie, his mother, and I think, "How did I get here?" Never in my wildest soothsayer-fantasy-fortune-teller-imagination-dreams did I think, at age fifty-six, that I would re-create my original family structure of two adults and three children. Kathie, me, her daughter Marissa, who is eleven, our son Forrest, who is five, and our new little Theo. Kathie always said that, even in high school, she knew she was going to have three children. What did I know I wanted in high school? What did I know I wanted now? I didn't know I wanted to live with Kathie until I lived with her. I didn't know I wanted to have a child until I first held him in my arms. I did think I wanted to end up one day living by the sea, but being a Gemini, I could never decide which ocean I wanted to end up by: I kept bouncing back and forth between coasts. Then, on my fifty-fourth birthday, Kathie surprised me by taking me to the American Hotel in Sag Harbor. She had never been out to Sag Harbor, and taking me there gave her a chance to see the place for the first time.

After dinner, at the lovely old American Hotel, we went out for a walk and came upon a large rambling Victorian house for sale. Kathie tried the front door and it was open, so we just walked in. It wasn't really breaking and entering. It was really just entering. We walked through the whole house fantasizing about what it would be like to raise a family there, what it would be like to live right in the heart of the village of Sag Harbor.

The following day we called the realtor whose number was on the *For Sale* sign. We called just to find out the price of the house. It was out of our range and there was too much that needed to be done to that house to get it into shape for us to live in. If we wanted to go through with this fantasy we needed a place that we could just move into.

Well, real estate agents aren't called "real" estate agents for nothing. Once they feel you as a fish on their line, they just "reel" you in, and to top it off, this agent just happened to be named Jan Hooks and she just happened to work for Harpoon Realty. We were hooked and harpooned all at once. So we started coming out to Sag Harbor to look at houses and the first weekend out we saw two houses that we both liked very much.

Because we liked both houses, we were torn. One of the houses was built in eighteen-forty and we were very much drawn to that one because of its age, but when we got inside, much of it didn't look that old because of all the new Sheetrock and recessed ceiling lighting that had been put in. Parts of the house's interior were very historic and other parts looked like a doctor's waiting room.

Also, the house was set rather low in the landscape, so not only did you have that sort of low swampy feeling but there were no views. In fact, the master bedroom was on the first floor and the window looked out onto a small back yard and a large overgrowth of bamboo.

The other house that Jan Hooks showed us was not as old. It was built in eighteen-ninety but it was set on a slight rise, a little hill, and that made all the difference. There were different cozy views from all the windows. Also, very little had been done to this house. It had those old wide-board pinewood floors and the doorways were at odd and crazy angles, as if the house had shifted over the years. We both loved this house right away. So did my best friend, Ken, who has a fine architectural eye. The only person who didn't like it—in fact, was rather freaked out by it—was my accountant and financial advisor. The first time he laid eyes on the house he advised me not to buy it, and when I insisted upon going ahead with the deal, he made me sign a notarized disclaimer that I would not hold him responsible when the house fell down.

As we got closer to going through with the purchase, more trepidation set in. We began to wonder about the school system. We had heard it was good, but what did we know? We wondered if we could survive the long, cold, gray winters. I wondered if I would miss New York City after thirty years there and not be able to live without that crazy hustle and bustle that had become such a natural part of my life. Kathie wondered if she could keep her newly founded talent agency so far from the city. Could she work out of this new home? It was a big move to contemplate for all of us. Our son Forrest was a real city kid, born in St. Vincent's Hospital, and so, to some extent, was Kathie's daughter, Marissa. She wasn't born in New York City but she sure did take to it when she moved there with her mother, when she was only three.

As for myself, I had a very odd reaction to moving to Sag Harbor. I had a fantasy that as soon as we moved in, I would come down with a vile case of hepatitis and not be able to get out of bed. Where I saw this hepatitis coming from was not polluted Long Island shellfish but rather one of those salad-bar delis in New York City, one of those places Kathie refers to as "the dirty deli" or "Dutefingers Deli." She won't eat at them. She's sure she will get sick. I do eat at them. I know I shouldn't, but I do, and my fantasy was that, just as I was about to escape at last from New York, after thirty years of relatively good health, I eat some salad fixed by a food handler who has just a little bit of poop under his fingernail and I come down with this bad case of hepatitis. In this fantasy, I see myself stretched out in our big cherrywood bed, stretched out there as yellow as a summer squash, and I see my stepdaughter, Marissa, of all people, trying to nurse me back to health. I see Marissa coming through the crooked doorway of the bedroom with a big, overflowing bowl of hot chicken soup. She has made this soup herself, and the soup is slopping over the edges and dripping through the cracks of the wide-board pinewood floors. It is dripping down through the cracks into the living room. Then, when the whole family is asleep, I see myself getting out of bed in a delirious state and wandering, in a late November wind and rain, in my long underwear across the street into the historic cemetery. I am headed for the old Whalers' Church, not for Jesus and the Twelve Disciples, but for their twelve-step program, one of the best in the country. Midway across that historic cemetery, where no one is allowed to be buried now, I fall down and perish. Kathie and the children come looking for me and find me there, lying dead beside the stone of Phoebe Niles, who died October 23, 1804, aged seventeen years eight months fifteen days. They find me and wrap me in two plastic garbage bags and give me a secret burial aside Phoebe Niles's tombstone, which reads:

Behold and see as you pass by
As you are now so once was I
As I am now so you must be
Prepare for death and follow me.

What a silly fantasy. Where did that come from? Did I make it up, or did it make me up? Well, let it go, because instead of death, when we move into the new house, new life comes. Kathie gets pregnant! Oh my God! How did that happen? I wonder. Another big surprise that plain freaks me out as much or more than the thought of being buried beside Phoebe Niles.

When I heard about this new pregnancy, I rushed in to my therapist, very upset, and told her, "I don't think I want this child, I have just adjusted to this almost new configuration of Kathie, me, Forrest, and Marissa. I really don't want to add someone new to this already complicated family structure." My therapist told me that I sounded clear about my feelings and that I should go and tell Kathie what I had just told her. I did just that. I ran to Kathie while what I had said to Martha, my therapist, was fresh in my mind. I ran right to Kathie and told her, "I don't think I want this child. I have just adjusted to the almost new configuration of you, me, Forrest, and Marissa."

Kathie was stunned and very hurt. I could tell she did not expect this response from me. I was amazed to see that she was ready to do my bidding with one condition. She said, "If this means that you don't want to have any more children, I am not going to use abortion as a form of birth control. I am not going to get two operations. I'm not going to get an abortion and have my tubes tied. If I abort this child, you're going to have to get a vasectomy." That's what she said to me, and I said I'd look into it. I'd look into getting a vasectomy.

I did look into it . . . a little bit . . . or just enough to come back to the bargaining table to suggest that maybe if we had an amniocentesis and found out that it was a girl, we could keep the baby. I told Kathie that I was afraid of having another boy because my father had three sons and I saw what we did to him.

Kathie came back with a big "No way! I don't play those kind of games with life."

The following week I had a breakthrough in therapy. When I started talking about the whole issue of abortion again, I suddenly started to cry, and through my tears I told Martha that I was too old to opt for death. I wanted to welcome new life into our family whether it was a girl or a boy. I was prepared to suffer the consequences.

So the decision was made and Martha remarked that I

seemed clear and told me to please remember this feeling of clarity so I could look back on it in the future when the going got rough.

After I had this breakthrough with Martha I rushed down the street to join Kathie and Rachel for our couple's therapy session. We were doing a whole lot of therapy over this issue. As soon as I walked in, I could see that Kathie was prepared for the worst. The room was filled with an air of gloom and then slowly, in an almost calculatedly withholding way, I sort of leaked the news of my change of mind. In spite of my emotionally tapped-down report on my decision to have the child, it was a very joyous moment for us all.

Friends and relatives were very supportive of our decision to have another child. The first slightly negative, not exactly supportive voice that we encountered came that summer on a beach in Martha's Vineyard. I was living in the Vineyard with my family while performing my monologue *It's a Slippery Slope* at the Vineyard Haven Playhouse and we were all on the beach one day along with Kathie's sister and her husband, who were visiting us from Stowe, Vermont. A man came up to us on the beach and said to me, "You look familiar," and I just said, "I am," which is the way I choose to respond when someone sort of recognizes me but is not sure if they have seen me on TV, in a film, or if I am one of their neighbors. So I just say, "I am," and leave it at that. I just say it and wait for their reaction. Now, this guy on the beach did not exactly think my cute response was funny. He said, "Oh no, I know where I've seen you. You're not a neighbor of mine in Providence, where I live. That's what I thought you were at first. No, you're the guy that did that *Slippery Slope* monologue at the Playhouse in Vineyard Haven. The monologue where you talk about marrying your girlfriend while you are having an affair, and then just after you get married, you make the woman you're having the affair with pregnant. Then you seem to have a nervous breakdown as a result of all of this when it really should be your new wife that was breaking down."

"Please," I said. "No more. I don't need a synopsis of what I already know too well and can't forget."

Then this guy on the beach looked over at Kathie, who was standing very pregnant at the water's edge while holding Forrest's hand, and he said, "Is that the woman you made pregnant?" I nodded yes and he said, "And she's pregnant again?" to which I nodded again yes, and then he said, "Well, my goodness, you really are going in for total immersion, aren't you?" Then he turned to me and said, "Do I look familiar to you?" to which I replied, "Not really." Then he introduced himself as Peter Kramer, the author of *Listening to Prozac*. Meanwhile, Kathie's sister, who was at a distance, thought he was Martin Short and was waving all during our conversation and calling out, "Hi! I just loved you in *Father of the Bride*."

Kathie was sure it was going to be a girl and we were going to name her Aliza Ann Gray. She was sure it was to be a girl because she didn't have morning sickness and she was carrying it higher, as she did with her daughter, Marissa. She was sure it was a girl because her grandfather had blessed her and said, "It's a girl." In New York City, street people touched her on the stomach and proclaimed, "It's a girl!" And she was craving peanut butter, just as she had with Marissa.

In preparation for the birth of this girl, we both had to go in for genetic counseling. This was new for both of us. We were required to take it because Kathie was thirty-five and I was . . . well I was ready for genetic counseling. I mean, I hadn't gone through it when we had our first son because I was married to someone else. That made life very complicated, so I was not there for the birth of my son.

Kathie and I were receiving our genetic counseling at the Southampton Hospital, where we were planning to have our baby girl delivered. The questions that were asked seemed mainly to do with our family histories of psychopathology rather than their physiopathology, and I was amazed at how much odd stuff came up. As for me, I'd been made so myopic by my mother's off-and-on madness and eventual suicide that I had never given much thought to the rest of my family tree. The more they probed and questioned me, the more I started to remember that my mother's mother, for instance, had a form of Tourette's. She would take these involuntary short breaths all the time, these little staccato inhales. She kept sucking her breath in at the end of her sentences. I'm sure it was a form of Tourette's, but she was a Christian Scientist, so no one really ever called attention to it. It was one of those unacknowledged, weird conditions that seemed to thrive in certain pockets of my family. She was clearly in denial. Oh, and then I remembered my grandmother's sister, my Great-aunt Sally, who lived alone in the wilds of Scituate, Rhode Island. She was a dowser and I think that's pretty much how she made a living, just going out dowsing for wells. She would cut a small apple-tree branch shaped like a wishbone and then, holding it with two hands, she'd wander around people's fields until the branch started to vibrate wildly and get pulled down to the earth by what felt like a magical force. After she did this, people would dig down and find well water very close to the surface of the ground. It was a remarkable phenomenon. I can remember standing behind Aunt Sally with my hands on her old hands and feeling the stick tremble all by itself and then just go down like a dart drawn to a bull's-eye.

Well, my Aunt Sally had her own brand of psychic disturbances during full moons. She'd get what I can only call "moonstruck." She would go into these strange wide-eyed trances and just sit, or sometimes wander, under the full moon. One time, when she was visiting her sister, my grandmother, who lived by Narragansett Bay, she filled her pockets with rocks and walked into the bay under a full moon. She just walked right into Narragansett Bay but she didn't sink and drown because her bloomers filled up with air. She just floated for a while under the full moon and then got out and walked home.

After dealing with me, the genetic counselor turned her questions onto Kathie and Kathie said, "Come to think of it, my mother has a brother down in San Antonio, Texas, who can't go out of the house because soda machines give him orders."

I just thought: Onward and upward. "There's nothing good nor bad but thinking makes it so."

I was very excited to be able to be there for the birth of our child and to maybe be able to help out a little. I had a strong feeling that this would be my first and last, so I was attentive in our birthing classes. For the first time in my life, I was a good student. I was also the oldest first-time father in the room. I was old enough to be the father of any of the other expectant parents.

Everything looked like and felt like it was going to be on schedule. The doctor told Kathie not to travel into the city anymore. I wasn't working at the time, so my schedule was wide open, but one of these surprise jobs came along just when you don't want them but you can't say no because it's too good an offer. Here's what happened: Fran Drescher, who plays the Nanny on TV, had gone to see my performance in Los Angeles and liked it so much she came up with an ingenious idea of having me play her therapist on her TV show. Fran even called my home directly. Kathie and I were out and our nanny at that time, Joan, answered the phone call from the TV nanny, and thought it was a joke. She turned out to be a great fan of *The Nanny* and just could not believe that she would be calling Sag Harbor. Well, Fran made me an offer I couldn't refuse and I just had to go. It really sounded like a fun job. Kathie and I both thought that baby Aliza would come before I had to tape *The Nanny*, but when she didn't come on the due date, we all got nervous. Would I be forced to miss the birth of my child because I was having to play a therapist on TV? I mean, I could not accept the fact that I would miss the real birth of my child for the fake reality of TV. But I also could not afford to give up the job. Then it happened, saved by the birth!

On January 16, at 3 a.m., Kathie started having her first contractions. There was a wild, wild storm raging outside as we rushed to get ready for the trip to the hospital. Snow had been forecast, but we were lucky to be hit with a big rain instead. It was a wild nor'easter that shook our house to its foundation. On the drive to the hospital, the whole landscape moved and twisted like a Currier & Ives Disney Fantasia dream. Then, when we got to the hospital, there was this odd mood in the air. There was a sense of tension like when we'd first come there in July for Kathie's amniocentesis. Before we went in, we took a walk on the beach in Southampton and spotted one lone man standing at the edge of the shore, looking out to the sea and crying. Kathie and I thought someone had drowned, and when we walked over to this man to see what was wrong, he proclaimed, "We can never fly safely again. Someone has blown up TWA flight 800 to Paris."

When we arrived at the Southampton Hospital for the amnio, the whole hospital was in a state of emergency. They were expecting survivors and bodies to be brought in at any moment.

The hospital was in another strange state and it wasn't the storm that was causing it. The head nurse warned us not to be concerned with the general mood of the nurses because, just an hour ago, there had been a stillborn and that always leaves a strange feeling in the air.

It was so very difficult for Kathie and me to imagine such a horrible thing happening to us or to anyone. I don't think either of us could really take in the fact of a stillborn. Also, Kathie's daughter, Marissa, was there and we both felt we had to protect her somehow. Marissa was only ten. Kathie had asked the hospital if she could bring her with us to witness the birth of our child, but the hospital discouraged it. They didn't think a ten-year-old could watch a baby being born without freaking out and running into the halls. But Kathie insisted. So we brought her with us and there she was, all ready to go, with her little throwaway camera in hand.

Kathie was quite confident that the birth of her third child would be smooth, short, and sweet. She had not been long in labor with the other two, and she was under the impression that it only gets easier and quicker with a third child. She was wrong. Eleven hours later, at three in the afternoon, with the storm raging, we were still at it. Kathie was in a lot of discomfort. The only position that felt right to her was on all fours. She knelt there on her hands and knees on that bed like a wild animal. I could tell that our two nurses were just a little bit bothered by this unorthodox posture. They assumed it did not come out of any birthing classes we had attended, and they were right.

Marissa had gotten some sleep in the waiting room and now she was groggy but up, wedged in the corner with her little camera. As for myself, I was amazed at how well I was doing in spite of the lack of air and the stuffiness. I was wide awake. I think part of my energy came from that raging nor'easter outside the window. It all, in a way, seemed so foreign yet so familiar. It was as if I were watching my mom give birth to me. I thought that had to do, perhaps, with the nurses' kind of local

Long Island accents. I think it had to do with their attitudes as well and, of course, the landscape, the view outside our window.

I made Kathie pregnant just after I married my girlfriend Ramona. When she refused to get an abortion, I broke off all contact with her. It was all rather complicated. The day Forrest was born, I was on the phone with my wife, and there was this call-interrupt signal and I took the call and it was Kathie's mother saying, "Congratulations! You are the father of a beautiful little boy!" When I switched back to my wife and she asked me who was on the line, I just told her it was a wrong number. What a mess!

Much later, when Kathie and I were speaking to each other again, Kathie told me how traumatized she was by Forrest's birth. He had taken a poop in the birth canal on his way out and swallowed it and some of it went down the wrong tube and into his lungs. The doctors just whisked him away to pump him out. Kathie was sure she had lost him as a fit punishment for the secret lusty-gusty way she had conceived him. I was spared all this trauma and knew nothing of it until later.

I can't imagine having a child in New York City. Perhaps that's why I never did before. I had always fantasized that if and when I had a child it would be in northern California. We, me and some sweet hippie beauty I was living with, would have a water birth or the child would be brought into the world by a midwife in a teepee somewhere. I always thought that one day it would all, at last, happen to me in northern California. In fact, I had begun to define my life as what I did while waiting to move to northern California. Now here I was in Southampton, Long Island, in the middle of a wild January nor'easter, trying to help a woman named Kathie give birth to our second child. When I wasn't helping her with her breathing, I was trying to pry free that hermetically sealed window in the room so we could get some air.

When Kathie at last felt the baby coming, I hardly had time to change into my scrubs and help the nurse roll Kathie onto her back. Now the doctor was there and Marissa was standing behind him, her little camera raised. One nurse had Kathie's left leg bent back at the knee and I was pushing back the other leg to help open her up. I think I was calm and doing real well, until I looked down and saw this strange bluish mass trying to push through. I remember at that moment I thought, oh my God, it looks like she is giving birth to a dead beaver. Then this beaver transformed into a hairy blue football and I thought, how is that ever going to fit through that little opening? And then pop! It was out and I cried, "Wow, look at the balls on that girl!"

Marissa was flashing away with her little camera while at the same time exclaiming, "Oh my God! I don't believe it!" Then when she looked down to see the surprise that she had, not a sister, but a brother instead, she exclaimed, "All right! Now I get my own room!" And I thought, "Oh no, death by boydom. They will take me down."

When my friend Ken was visiting us in Sag Harbor, Kathie and I had the National Public Radio news on in the background, as we often do. Both Ken and I were kind of half listening to it at the same time that we were talking to each other, so the radio became a kind of ambient background chatter. One day I heard something about William Burroughs at eighty-one years old. We both heard some mumble-jumble about Burroughs at eighty-one, and Ken said, "Oh my God, William Burroughs has finally died at eighty-one." And I said, "Oh my God, he almost outlived my father, and what a life he had." Then Ken turned up the radio and we heard that William Burroughs was not dead at eighty-one but, rather, he was having an art opening in Los Angeles at eighty-one. And I said, "Oh my God, Ken, how does he do it? He had wild sex with over three hundred Arab boys, shot his wife dead in the head, and was addicted to heroin for most of his adult life, and now he's having an art opening at eighty-one? My dad died at eighty-one." And Ken just said, "Yeah, but William Burroughs didn't have three sons."

There he was, my second son, with his attached umbilical cord snaking out of him and into Kathie. There he was, stunned and half reclining in the doctor's arms. There he was, Theo. That's what we chose to call him in case she was a he. Theo, short for nothing. Short for the study of God. Theo Spalding Gray. T. S. Gray. I just looked down at him and saw this big WHY? expression coming back at me. He seemed to be asking me, why this? Why something and not nothing? I totally empathized with this expression. At the same time, I knew I wasn't a mirror to him. He'd not been in the world long enough to take this big WHY? expression off of me. This WHY?, this little perplexed scowl that was coming back at me, I could totally relate to. He had clearly brought this into the world with him and I just looked down at him and thought, oh little one, oh sweet one, you may already have spent the best days of your life in there.

I cut the umbilical cord and the crimson blood sprayed. I bent down and kissed Kathie and cried. At the same time, I couldn't help recalling that line from *Waiting for Godot*: "They give birth astride of a grave, the light gleams an instant, then it's night once more."

As soon as we all recuperated from Theo's birth, we thought of Forrest and how much we wished he could have been there for the event. He was waiting at home with his baby-sitter, Joan, and we called him to tell him that he had a brother. He seemed very calm and matter-of-fact. I told him I was coming to get him right away and I did. The twenty-five-minute drive to Sag Harbor seemed to happen in a flash. The storm had passed and a warm amber late-afternoon January light illuminated what was left of that glorious farmland on the back roads between Southampton and Sag Harbor. I felt like a happy man, a very happy man, as I drove.

Forrest seemed more excited when I picked him up.

While we drove back to the hospital, he told me how happy he was to have a brother, because now they could form a great girl-hating club together, which could also include me if I wanted.

When we got to the hospital, the head nurse told me that Kathie had been moved to her room and Marissa was there with her. On the way to her room, Forrest and I had to pass the nursery. All the infants were in their cribs, except for one, who was on permanent display on what looked like a raised examination table. Forrest and I both stopped to look at this baby, and as we looked, we both knew it was Theo. Forrest had never seen him before, and I hardly had, but we both knew at the same time that it was Theo. Forrest stood there for a long time, just staring at that startled flailing newborn brother of his.

Marissa was in Kathie's room, reading *Teen People*, and Kathie seemed just fine for someone who had been through eleven hours of labor. Her only problem was her roommate, who was turning out to be a real bitch. She actually accused Kathie of stealing her hospital-supplied maxi-pads out of the shared bathroom, and she kept the TV on until 4 a.m.

When Theo was brought to Kathie, we had our new focus. I was amazed at how fascinated I was by this—by all objective standards—ugly newborn. Before I had children, I was the typical cynic, thinking the earth is overpopulated by a stupid, unconscious, polluting disease called humanity. Or, we have made such a mess of the world, who in their right mind would want to bring a child into it? Now all this was wiped away by this child we were calling Theo—a basic miracle.

Kathie had made plans with the hospital to have a tubal ligation the day after Theo was born. With all the excitement, I had forgotten about this. She was supposed to have the operation in the afternoon, but in the morning they came to her room to tell her they had an opening for the operation right then and would she like it? She said yes and had the procedure done. Kathie is not a great procrastinator. She does not sit on situations and think about them. I do. I ruminate and speculate and live out the alternative actions and their fantasy consequences, in my mind, over and over again. In fact, if I am guilty of anything, it is living in my head more with the world that never was and never will be than I am in the world that is. Kathie lives more in the world that is. So, when she called to tell me that she had just had her tubes tied, I responded with surprise and then said something like, "I'm not so sure now." Which of course was the absolutely wrong thing to say. Needless to say, Kathie got very upset.

When I hung up the phone, I tried to forgive myself for my ambivalence. I went for my six-mile bike ride and thought, as I rode, I must forgive myself for not knowing what I wanted. For me, that is a natural state of mind because I am only living once. There is nothing, no other life, of mine to compare this one to. There is no way of knowing what the right decision in life is if you have no other life to compare it to. We are like blind people backing into the future, living for better or for worse lives only once, and so on.

It was the children who finally got me out of New York City. It was the children who led to what I call the double-chaos factor. Over a thirty-year period, I'd lived in the city with three different women. With the first two women, Liz and Ramona, I did not have children. These two women helped me make a quiet nest where we could work and make art together. The creative act was our focus and not family and children.

It's funny how New York City is so conducive to keeping some people in a holding pattern of arrested adolescence. If you don't make a lot of money, and try to live in New York City, you end up in a small space in a crowded city with little to spend on family life. If you continue to live in that situation for a long time, you either get out of it or get rather addicted to the traumatic chaos of that crazy city. I was happy to go out and experience all the chaotic creative stimulation of New York as long as I could limp back to a nurturing woman and our quiet little nest together. I was content to cope with the city and be in pursuit of art either as an observer or as a practitioner. But when I had children, just two at that time, Forrest and my stepdaughter, Marissa, I was overwhelmed by what became the double chaos. The chaos was both in the streets and in the home. I had no place to run to. I had to get out.

When I first came to New York City for a one-week visit in December of 1959, I had been reading all those big, fat books of Thomas Wolfe's and I went up to the top of the Riverside Cathedral bell tower and looked out over Manhattan and made a pledge that, like Thomas Wolfe, I would someday come to live there and be "a writer."

When I finally moved to the city in 1967 I was so overwhelmed by it that I couldn't even begin to think about writing about it. It was the outrageous chaos and absurd random juxtaposition of strangenesses that knocked me out. New York for me was what I could only call a functioning city right on the edge of dysfunction, a case of functional/dysfunction. It was always on the edge of not working but, for some mysterious, almost miraculous reason, it did not totally break down. Maybe this is because it never stops. Maybe that's why it keeps on working, because it's always going twenty-four hours a day, and if it stopped for as much as a minute, it might never start up again.

When I first came to New York, the city reminded me of a poster that my mom had framed in our bedroom. On the poster was a picture of a bumblebee, followed by a bold-print title that read, **THE BUMBLEBEE CANNOT FLY**, and underneath this caption:

> *According to all aerodynamic laws*
> *the bumblebee's body size and weight*
> *in relationship to the size of its wings*
> *would make it impossible for it to fly.*
> *But ignoring these laws,*
> *The bumblebee flies anyway.*

That, for me, was New York City. All human logic seems to say a city that size crammed on a little island should not work, but it does. It is a very miraculous place.

Because Forrest was born in New York, he is still a kid of the city. I remember how I tried to wean Forrest off New York. When he was not quite two and a half I took him with me out to Esalin Institute in Big Sur, California, where I was running a storytelling workshop. Some people think of Big Sur, California, as Paradise on Earth, and I wanted to expose Forrest to it at an early age. When we got there he was so bothered by the earth and grass that he wouldn't let me put him down. He ran from flowers. Then when we got up to Berkeley he just jumped down out of my arms onto the concrete and ran. He was so happy. He ran all the way down Telegraph Avenue, shining his flashlight in the eyes of all the homeless there. He's still not been taken over by the slow rhythms of Sag Harbor. In fact, I like to go back to New York with Forrest to visit so we can reexperience that chaotic city together. Not long ago, we went to see the *David Copperfield Magic Show* on Broadway. Forrest and I were traveling by subway from SoHo up to Forty-fifth Street. On our way to the subway, we came upon a man sitting with a big telescope and, for only two dollars, you could look through his telescope and see Saturn with its rings. Both Forrest and I looked through it. I'd never seen Saturn and its rings before, and so clear. It was fantastic! There we were gazing at Saturn and its rings for the first time together, on the corner of West Broadway and Spring Street.

A little farther up West Broadway, we ran into an old man dressed in a pin-striped suit, bent over a little Casio, playing requests from passersby. To my amazement, Forrest requested "Hot Cross Buns" and the old man played it. Then on the subway a woman came into our car crying out, "My daughter was burned in the hotel fire! Sixty percent of her body burned! Shortly after that, I got the gangrene and lost three toes." Then she pointed down at her foot and cried, "See, see for yourself, the three toes I'm missing!" Sure enough, she had cut a piece of her shoe off so you could see her bare foot and the missing toes. It was no doubt partly an act, but it was a good act and it deserved some money. I gave Forrest some money to give to her.

As soon as she exited our subway car, four street dancers entered and, putting their boom box on the floor just a few feet from Forrest and me, they began to break-dance up a storm. They were moonwalking. They were doing the rocking-horse rock. They were swinging around the subway poles and hanging from the straps. Forrest and I were stunned. What a show, and what great seats. Then we got to the *David Copperfield Show* and it was . . . well, it was . . . good, too. It was just a different kind of show.

Now Theo wakes beside me like my double son. My son. My sun. He's two sons/suns in one. Kathie and I are both amazed at how this little guy sleeps the whole night through. I was prepared, by our birthing class, to be woken every four hours, and then when Theo didn't wake me, I woke up every four hours anyway and put my ear on his chest just to hear if he was still alive and breathing. He seemed so fragile and barely in this world.

Now he's up, he has pulled himself up on the back of the bed and is looking out our north window. He's looking out and down the street to the Baptist church and the white picket fences that line the street on the way to the village. Now Kathie is awake beside him and she is asking and repeating her morning ritual question of, "Where's the light, Theo? Where's the light?" Theo is smiling that toothless grin that makes him look so old, that makes him look like the little old Italian winemaker that used to be on the Italian Swiss Colony wine bottle, and he is just so bright and happy to be alive.

I scramble to get up, determined to shower and get my yoga done before the other children come downstairs. I get up and leave Kathie to round up Forrest and Marissa. Because they are new to the house, Forrest and Marissa haven't really taken on regular sleeping places yet. Marissa was supposed to get her own bedroom in the attic, but the contractors Kathie called haven't shown up yet. Another condition that keeps Marissa and Forrest trying different beds in the guest room, Kathie's office, or at either end of the attic, is the fact that our house, by all reports but mine, seems to be haunted. Marissa heard a tea party going on in the living room at 3:30 a.m. one night. Forrest has seen the eyes of the unfinished Gilbert Stuart portrait of George Washington we have hanging over the fireplace follow him. Then, just the other day, he came to me quite panic-stricken to report that one of George's eyes winked at him. Kathie has clearly heard a solid five-stroke knocking in the attic when no one was up there. At first she thought it was Marissa sleepwalking or moving around. Then she got up to check on the kids and found Forrest asleep in the guest room and Marissa sleeping on the couch in her office. I am the only one who hasn't had a visitation yet, but I am open to it. Sometimes I wake in the middle of the night and just lie there listening. I don't think I could sleep alone in our house, but then, I haven't had that opportunity yet, and I doubt that I ever will.

I go to shower, and, looking down into the bathtub, I see a scattered army of plastic action figures. The whole bottom of the tub is littered with them. Never did I think it would come to this. I remember when I was having the affair with Kathie and I'd go in to use her toilet and I'd look down into her bathtub and see the litter of plastic objects that three-year-old Marissa had left there. I saw everything from naked headless Barbie dolls to miniature plastic sinks and dishwashers, and I remember thinking, that's one good reason not to have children. Now I'm looking down at my son Forrest's mess. It's like I don't have any of my own space anymore. It's like I have been invaded. It is as weird to me, as much an unexpected surprise, as our new green Volvo station wagon piled with stuff from floor to ceiling, four bikes on the back, and three squabbling children in the back seat, one of us driving while the other referees.

I don't bother to clear the action figures but just step into the middle of Ninja Turtles, Space Jam, Buzz Lightyear, Darth Vader, Freexe, Luke Skywalker, Spider-Man, R2D2, the Jurassic Park Rage Rig, Sharptooths, Longnecks, and all the Power Rangers, Billy, Kimberly, Tommy, and Adam as they all float up and dance around my naked ankles like a Busby Berkeley plastic cartoon water ballet.

Down in the living room, I do my first yoga stretches as I also look around at that room I love so. It's about thirty feet long by twenty-five feet wide but it's our first real living room and we all love it. It has a long comfortable couch and two colonial wing-backed chairs on either side of the fireplace. The carpet I am doing my yoga on was randomly selected by my friend Ken's keen, quick, over-the-shoulder artistic eye. I had brought him into ABC Carpet in New York City to help me make a decision on one of two rather busy traditional Oriental carpets that Kathie and I had picked out. We could not decide between the two and Ken, to my surprise, didn't like either. He said, "I'd more likely go for . . ." Then he looked around and just pointed randomly to one of the carpets on top of a pile. "Maybe something like that one." He was right on. He found it just like that. It was a more solid carpet and not as busy as the other two. It had a more lyrical open pattern with plenty of space to breathe. It was not so geometrically claustrophobic. So now I do my yoga on it, on this, my magic flying carpet, and sometimes think of Ken and his fine, arty eye.

There are two major *George Washingtons* in the room, both of which Kathie bought in thrift shops. They're somehow just right for the room. They are both a little campy and a little patriotic-real. There's the large copy of the unfinished Gilbert Stuart over the mantel that I mentioned, and then there's *George Washington on His Deathbed*, which hangs over the couch. George is in bed with all that eighteenth-century soft busy ruffle around him, all those endlessly pleated fabrics that used to collect all sorts of germs. And there he is dying and looking not so much like he's dying. His head is raised in a sort of alert, panicked, inquisitive attitude, as if to say what, after all I went through at Valley Forge, dying from just a cold? Beside him kneels one weeping woman, who I assume is Martha. Then standing, one at his side and one at the end of the bed, are two head-in-hand professional men. Maybe they're doctors or a lawyer and a doctor, I'm not sure. Let's just say two "professional people" as opposed to "emotional people." A slight distance behind them in a doorway stand two wide-eyed but indifferent slaves who really look like two white men in blackface. It's a busy picture with a lot going on. I just can't stop looking at it.

At the far end of the living room are the French doors, which open onto a small yard. These were, no doubt, a relatively new addition to this eighteen-nineties house, but what a great addition they are. It's like having a glass wall. All that light saves me from the morning doldrums.

Now, as I do my first yoga stretches, I look to my right out the window to the left of the fireplace and see the church steeple of what I think is one of the local Catholic churches. There are, I think, as many churches as there are bars in Sag Harbor. This particular church steeple is a favorite of mine because of the way it captures and reflects the day's changing light. Now, as I look at it, I see it capturing the rose light of the progressing sunrise.

I really do love the churches from the outside, I think, as I stretch, doing my yoga. I'm not really sure what goes on inside them, but I do love the outside architecture. They are for me like giant, elegant birdhouses. As a Christian Scientist, I never got to go to church. My brothers and I only went to Sunday school. The Christian Science church requires that you attend Sunday school until you are twenty-one. I guess this is because it takes such a long education before you can understand what the first reader is reading about in church when they read from Mary Baker Eddy's *Science and Health with Key to the Scriptures*. I never made it to church because I dropped out of Christian Science by the time I was seventeen. I dropped out and fell into the world of doubt.

I do remember that once, during Cub Scouts Sunday, I got to attend what we called, in Barrington, the Red Church. It was called the Red Church because it was made of red brick. I think the denomination was High Episcopalian, which for me at the time seemed right next door to Catholic, which for us Christian Scientists was a no-no. We had been taught that the Catholics were pagan idolaters who worshipped graven images. We used to snicker when we saw them cross themselves before going in swimming. Well, I say "we" but there were really only my brothers and I and a couple of other brothers who were Christian Scientists in Barrington. We were definitely a minority.

Then, of course, there was a big attraction to our pagan opposites. When my brother Rocky grew up and one summer became a group leader for International Living in Chile, he didn't come back for three years and fell in love with the place and also with a Chilean Catholic, whom he came very close to marrying. I remember how distraught my mother and her mother were when they got the news. I remember my grandmother said, "Oh dear, Jesus, no. He's going to the Wow Wows!" At the time, I thought that Wow Wows must be some transformation of "bow wows" as in "going to the dogs." As for my mom, she prayed earnestly every morning that Rocky would be guided back to the fold.

Those Italian American Catholic girls from the other side of the tracks were real exotic to me. I didn't dare tell Mom about them. Whenever I was around them in school, I'd get all weak in the knees. I was always a little overwhelmed by their sensuality and that exotic smell of garlic on their breath. My mother never cooked with garlic, so I didn't recognize the odor. In fact, I thought the smell of garlic was really the smell of the wafers the Catholics received at Communion. I had attended Mass on one Cub Scout outing and saw some of the girls from my class at school come to the altar, bow down, and eat that mysterious wafer. I remember the way they stuck their tongues out to receive it, like little vipers, ooh la la. And look, now I've come full circle and made a family with one, or at least partially one, because Kathie Russo is Irish/Italian American. She is definitely a Catholic in the sense that once a Catholic always a Catholic. She does cross herself before we take off on a plane, and I no longer snicker at that. I say, try it all, anything and everything, to help keep us safe. The only issue I had problems with was Kathie's desire to get our two sons baptized. I mean, I understand her need but don't really feel I could be a part of it. Kathie felt that because she and Marissa were baptized and the boys had not been, she might end up in heaven without them. (I was a little hurt that she would not miss me there.) I thought this was a noble sentiment and told her she should go ahead with it on her own, but she wanted it to be a family thing and hoped to have it done in the First Presbyterian Church, also known as the old Whalers' Church. Then I gave it some consideration and thought I'd at least look into it with her, so we invited the minister of the church to come to our house and talk to us about what had to be done in order to have the boys baptized. It turned out to be pretty complicated. It involved some indoctrination and group initiation in which we all had to publicly accept Jesus Christ as our Lord and Saviour. I was sure I wouldn't know how to do this and I wanted to go back to our original idea of having John Perry Barlow (self-ordained minister, ex-Grateful Dead lyricist and cognitive, distant cyber-space cowboy) baptize them in the ocean. I just didn't see how I could accept Jesus until I found him, and I wasn't even looking. That takes me back to that Cub Scouts Sunday outing when I was looking for Jesus. I was searching with all my being.

I remember that Sunday so well—the first time when

at last I entered a real done-up stained-glass-windowed, felt-pewed church. I'd never been in anything like that before, and here I was, in my Cub Scout outfit, kneeling on a velvet-covered kneeler and praying with all my might to God. It's not that I hadn't prayed before (Mom led us in silent prayer every night at the dinner table), but I had never prayed in such a highly ritualized setting. I think I thought on that Sunday that if I prayed hard enough, God would give me a recognizable sign. I mean, if it was gonna happen, wasn't that the place? I remember feeling so constipated as I knelt there, like I was straining on the pot but nothing came. All I could feel was a giant emptiness inside.

As I go into my next yoga stretch, my eye moves from the steeple to the trees just outside the window on the other side of our privet hedge. Ahh, trees, I think. How had I lived so long without trees? Thirty years in New York City without one tree in view. Had I been punishing myself? And for what? What was I doing penance for? Thirty years without trees, and now I had them. Looking out my window now, I see this one tree that I think might be an elm and it reminds me of all those beautiful elms I grew up with on Rumstick Road in Barrington, where we lived in a little clapboard Victorian. In summer, Rumstick Road was a long green shady tunnel of elms. It was all thick with leaves on graceful black, twisting trunks. Those slender, curving, splaying, gracefully twisting trunks made, for me, the most beautiful trees in the world. They were like dancing bodies in the wind. In winter, after a beautiful autumn of running and jumping through billowing white smoke from piles of burning elm leaves, I would see the trees become like great long dark vocal cords to the cold breath of winter wind. We would run screaming from our neighbor's house through the snow to our house, screaming under the ferocious roar of the winter wind through those dark elms. I think now of my older brother, Rocky, and how he loved those trees and wanted to be a tree surgeon when he grew up. Then I remember one day he brought me the *Providence Journal* to show me those headlines:

WORST ECOLOGICAL DISASTER TO STRIKE NORTH AMERICA

The Dutch Elm Disease wiped out ninety-five percent of America's elms. We watched them die and we watched the tree surgeons and the town workers come to cut them down. We no longer recognized our town. It was as though we were living in some treeless Southwestern cowboy town. Rumstick Road was flat and naked of trees.

It was around that time, I remember, that my brother Rocky began to act up, or "act out," as they might say today. He gave my father some real problems. I don't know if it had to do with all the Dutch elms being cut down, or if it just had to do with the restlessness of puberty, but Rocky suddenly wanted to drop out of high school and become a lumberjack in Maine. He would try to run away from home and hitchhike to Maine and he would do it in the most dramatic way. Instead of just walking out the front door, he would climb out his bedroom window and make his way along a rain gutter, then shinny down a pine tree. It would take him hours just to get as far as the Massachusetts border, where the state police usually picked him up and took him to the station. They would call my father, who had to get out of bed at two o'clock in the morning and head out to pick Rocky up and bring him home. Then Rocky would do it again and it started to be like this runaway routine.

When my father wouldn't let Rocky quit high school and go to Maine, he got himself thrown out. He poured hydrochloric acid into the tropical fish tank in biology class. When he was thrown out of Barrington High

School for doing this, he just hung around the house all day. He still wanted to go to Maine to become a lumberjack, and instead he stole a whole bunch of lumber from some of the new neighborhood construction sites. He took that lumber and built a small shack in the yard behind our house. He would kind of live out there, dressed in his L.L. Bean red-and-black plaid wool shirt. He would live out there eating Amazo instant chocolate pudding, which he'd whip up himself with water from our outdoor well and Mom's egg beater.

Thinking back on it now, I remember my father handled it well. My father was not a man who inflicted corporal punishment on his sons. He never hit us once. I think Dad felt that living and dying in this world was punishment enough. So corporal punishment was not his thing, but more sophisticated, creative punishments were. Dad went to the Barrington Department of Public Works and requested that they bring over some of the elm trees they cut down on Rumstick Road and pile them up in our back yard. It was an incredible sight I will never forget. Some of those elm-tree trunks were thirty and forty feet long and they were real thick and made a high pile such as you might see on the back of a lumber truck in northern Maine. My father just took from out of our barn an old handsaw that had belonged to my

Grandfather Horton and handed it to Rocky and said, "You want to be a lumberjack? Well, there you are. Start cutting." And he did. Rocky was out there every day cutting away and I thought, we will have firewood for a lifetime. At the same time, I didn't realize how fast things would change. How all those trees would never be cut and how Rocky would soon graduate magna cum laude from Brown University.

I look back at that as a wise move on my father's part. He helped my brother Rocky work through one of his fantasies. My first odd occupational fantasy surfaced when I was about fifteen years old. I was in vocational training in junior high and we had to select an occupation we thought we wanted to work at when we grew up. Once we selected it, we had to write a report on it. We had all these little pamphlets to guide us. There were little booklets that would give you information about what you had to do to become an accountant, a florist, the manager of a supermarket, or a truck driver. I think the teacher was trying to condition us to be service people for the town. I had been tossed in with a lot of kids who were going to quit school as soon as they reached sixteen. They would drop out and start working at service jobs. You see, I had failed seventh-grade math and had to repeat the whole of seventh grade—all my subjects. I also had a real difficult time with reading. I think I had a learning disability, a form of dyslexia. But no one knew what to call that kind of problem then. Because of this, they just referred to me as "slow," and I came to think that maybe that was how I got obsessed with becoming a member of the Ferrari racing team. Quite simply, I wanted to be "fast!"

Of course, my vocational-training teacher did not have any pamphlets on how to become a race-car driver for the Ferrari racing team, so I made up my own pamphlet, modeling it on my new hero, the Marquis de Portago, who had been written up in *Life* magazine because the car he was driving in the Italian millemiglia had a blowout and crashed into a crowd of people, killing himself and seven others.

As soon as I got my driver's license, I began to practice taking sharp turns with the family car, which was a 1954 Ford and did not have a very low center of gravity. Then in late September I was executing a very sharp turn on a wet day on Colts Drive in Bristol, right at the edge of Narragansett Bay. The car skidded on wet leaves, flipped and rolled, ending up on its side just inches from plunging into the bay. I was knocked unconscious and would have drowned had the car rolled in. When my father got back from looking at the wrecked car, my mother asked him what it looked like and he said, "Like the boy who was driving it should be dead."

At that moment, I really didn't know if he wanted me dead because he was so angry or was thankful that I was still alive. But he did not punish me. He did not punish me in a corporal way or in any other way. He left me pretty much on my own to punish myself, which I've done a very good job of over the years. I have to give Dad credit for controlling his anger. Being a father now, I know how hard that is.

It's here I have to confess that I hit my son Forrest just once. I was not in control. I see now how a father could easily lose control and hit his child. Just before Forrest turned three, Kathie and I took him on a trip to the west coast of Ireland and we were having a lovely time because the sun came out one day. This made it warm enough to go to the beach and swim. It was really a magnificent setting for a perfect moment. In some ways I was living through my son and the way he enjoyed the simple purity of that place. It was as if I was going back, through him, to Sakonnet, Rhode Island, to when I was his age in 1944. That whole Irish landscape was so rural, pristine, and undeveloped, just as Sakonnet was for me as a child. Bright green, sunlit fields. Lazy black-and-white dairy cows grazing. There were no houses in sight.

Then there was the turbulent brilliant blue Atlantic crashing in. Forrest was playing naked in a tidal pool. Kathie was jogging up and down on that vast beach, and I was running in and out of the waves like a little kid.

Finally, unable to resist Forrest naked in that tidal pool, I ran to him and took him in my arms and began to spin him around and around. Just as I was spinning into a perfect bonding moment, I looked down at my thighs, and to my horror I saw these awful blue, green, and purple bruises. This made me go right into a freakish panic. And to feed the panic, as I often do, I pulled up more fuel from my memory bank. In an instant, I recalled a story that was told me at my Esalin storytelling workshop by a woman about losing her right leg to cancer. Right there, at that moment, with little Forrest naked in my arms, I remembered her saying, "I first knew something was very wrong with my leg when I saw those horrid green-and-purple bruises." At that moment, I just collapsed into the tidal pool with stunned Forrest in my arms. Kathie came running over, crying, "What's wrong?" I looked up from the pool with Forrest still in my arms and said, "Oh my God, I got the leg cancer." Kathie just said, "Oh no you don't. You mean you still can't let yourself take a vacation? You're still punishing yourself? And for what? We are going right to a doctor now. I am not going to let you spoil this vacation."

We found a doctor in Galway and I immediately liked him because the first thing he said when we walked into his office was, "Well, I don't know you and you don't know me, so there's no sense in trustin' each other right off." And he went on to say, "So you think you have the leg cancer, then? Well, I wouldn't be so sure. We'll have to do a blood workup to read your platelet count and check on your clotting factor. It will take about three days to get the results, so for three days you know you're not going to die, so go have a party. Have a ball."

He was right! That doctor lifted the fear of death right off my shoulders and put it in the laboratory for a rest. My death was on temporary hold in some Irish blood lab. Death was at bay, and I was in this new joyous bubble with Kathie and Forrest. We had a great time. We went on a long canoe trip on the river just outside Galway. We had a great time, but toward the end of the third day, after spinning straw into gold, I heard the voice of Rumpelstiltskin reminding me that I had to call the doctor for the blood report. When we got back to the hotel I didn't have the courage to do it. I said, "Kathie, you call him, please. I'm going down to the bar for a Guinness." But Kathie said, "No, you know the doctor won't give me any information about you over the phone. He'll want to talk to you directly." I said, "Maybe not in Ireland. Maybe in Ireland it's different." And I left Kathie with Forrest to go down to the bar for a Guinness and a Jameson's neat. When I came back into the room, Kathie said, "I called the doctor and he said that you must call him yourself." I felt the fear, the real solid fear, and I felt faint. I sat down on the bed and said, "Oh my God, I think I'm going to be sick." And Kathie said, "Just kidding. Thought I'd give you a taste of your own medicine. But the doctor does want you to call him. He has good news but he also wants to talk to you about something."

I called and the doctor told me he was happy to report that my blood was healthy, but what he wondered about was Forrest, whom he called "the wee one." He said, "I saw you had a wee one, a little fellow with you. Is there any chance that he could be hitting or knocking on you in any way that you might have forgotten?"

Then wham! It hit me. But of course!

I had been reading D. W. Winnicott, the British child therapist, and I read about his theory that two- and three-year-olds often have an omnipotent fantasy that they can devour and destroy their parents. Winnicott feels that children are sometimes traumatized by this fantasy to the extent that they have to try to act it out in order to test it. I thought Forrest had been doing that to me. He had been biting my thighs and I was letting him do it as hard and as much as he wanted, just to prove he couldn't consume me. I hadn't noticed what he was doing until the good weather came and I changed into my bathing suit. That's when I saw the bruises.

Then, when we got back to America, Forrest was still at it, but he was a little taller, and instead of biting my thigh he just took a big gnashing bite right into my right testicle. I hauled off and smacked him almost at the same time he bit me. There was no rational process involved. I just had a ball-jerk reaction. I mean, he drew blood, my underwear was bloody!

As soon as he started to cry, I grabbed him and held him and told him how sorry I was and how much I loved him. At the same time I was thinking: What would drive him to do a thing like that? Was it early Oedipal? Will we ever really know? I doubt it.

Forrest is down from whatever bed he slept in last night. Forrest is down interrupting my yoga with his *Where's*

Waldo in Hollywood? book. He's asking me to pick Waldo out from what looks like about five hundred *Ben-Hur* extras. I'm telling him to get a magnifying glass and please wait until I've finished my yoga.

Forrest runs off in search of a magnifying glass and Kathie comes down with the portable radio playing the morning news. She's got the little yellow radio in her right hand and Theo wrapped in her left arm. She goes into the kitchen to put Theo in his high chair while I finish my yoga.

Kathie calls out to Forrest, who is looking for a magnifying glass, "What do you want for breakfast, sweetie?"

"*Cap'n Crunch!*" he yells back.

Marissa is down, boiling water for her instant oatmeal. I am amazed that both children got up on their own. They must have gotten to sleep before eleven o'clock last night. "Marissa, don't carry that boiling water near the baby," Kathie warns.

Then to Forrest Kathie says, "What do you want for lunch, dear?"

Forrest replies, "Peanut butter and jelly. No crusts on the bread, no peanuts in the butter, and no seeds in the jelly."

I, in the other room, am just finishing my salute to the sun, when I hear Kathie call to Marissa, who has gone out to the front porch to get the morning paper so she can search for any information about the Spice Girls, and I am amazed how much the newspaper is reporting about them. "Do you want me to put last night's pizza in your lunch bag?"

From the porch, Marissa yells back, "No, I saw a fly throw up on it last night!"

"What do you want for lunch, then?" Kathie calls back.

To which Marissa replies, "Tuna fish with celery chopped up in it."

Then Kathie discovers Marissa's uneaten tuna sandwich from the day before and says, "But, Marissa, you didn't eat your sandwich from yesterday. Why not?"

To which I hear Marissa reply, "I saw a bug on the lettuce." Now I'm groaning from the living room, thinking how much of the children's leftover food I'm going to have to eat. Then Kathie yells out to me from the kitchen, "Spalding, please finish up your yoga and go down to the cellar and get Forrest's jeans. They're hanging on the drying rack."

I complete my salute to the sun and go down to the cellar in search of Forrest's jeans. While fumbling around in the basement I hear that someone named Marissa has turned off the news on the radio and put on a Spice Girls

CD instead. She's playing "Wannabe" top-blast. I am outraged. I feel I'm living under a disco. I feel I'm about to have whiskey and a cigarette for breakfast. I yell, "Shut that thing down! Shut that damn thing down!" Then, from the cellar, I hear a big crash of glass and then a silence. Then I hear Forrest call down to me, "Dad, you know that picture of George Washington on his deathbed? Well, he's dead."

I rush upstairs from the cellar to find Kathie already in the living room taking command and reprimanding Marissa. Marissa's doing her old defense routine. "It was an accident. It was an accident, Mom. I really don't know how to dance in clogs."

Totally exasperated, Kathie yells, "They are my clogs and you are not to wear them! You don't do ballet steps in clogs, Marissa. Oh my God, my baby. Look at the mess. Glass all over the couch. Theo, my baby, is going to get into it. Get the vacuum cleaner! Marissa, go upstairs and gather up your homework while I vacuum the couch!"

By now I have handed Forrest his jeans and it turns out that they are too damp for him and he starts complaining, "I'm not going to be the only one in school with damp jeans."

"Throw them in the dryer!" Kathie yells to me like a

female ship's captain in a storm. "And help me get Marissa out of here."

It's a mad scramble, as if everyone is running to get off the sinking ship. Kathie finishes vacuuming the glass, grabs Marissa, grabs Marissa's knapsack, lunch, and sweater, and she's out the door and gone.

I am left with the boys. The house is now two people calmer. Now it's my turn to get Forrest ready for school and then Kathie or I will take him there, depending on which parent he chooses. I need to take Forrest up to the attic, where his bureau is with all his clothes. He's afraid to go up to the attic alone because I made the mistake of letting him see the *Chucky* video. Now he is afraid all his toys will come alive and give him the evil Chucky eye. So that means I'll have to climb the two flights of stairs with him and with Theo in my arms. I take Theo out of the high chair and, lifting him up into my arms, I am suddenly still and at peace. Oh, the blessed weight of a child, of this child. The way he cuddles and fits into my body like a part of me. At that moment I think the world is doomed to overpopulation. No wonder people keep having babies, just to keep on holding them.

As I start across the kitchen to follow Forrest up, I can feel and hear Theo's discarded Cheerios crunch on the floor under my feet.

Up in the attic now, with Theo in my arms, I gaze out one of my two favorite windows. They are the arched attic windows with a high view and through the first one, looking north, I can see a patch of the bay, now that so many of the leaves are down. Yes, one could say that, from late autumn to early spring, we have a partial water view. Then I move to the second arched window to look southeast over the cemetery. As we are closer to Halloween now, it reminds me of what my friend Howie said when he first laid eyes on that historic cemetery. He said, "What's that? A Halloween installation?" And yes, it does sometimes look unreal, or just too perfect. But I love it and can't stop looking at it. Now, turning, I see that Forrest has put on his own shirt and I blurt out, "Oh honey, you look . . ." and I stop because I almost say "beautiful," which is no longer allowed in the house as an adjective for Forrest. "Cool" is the new word. Everything is "cool." I will reluctantly accept "cool," but I won't let the word "awesome" into the house, not until something awesome happens, and we are waiting.

Downstairs, in the kitchen, we all greet Kathie, who is back from driving Marissa to school. It's just a short trip. The children could walk to school if we only took the time to teach them. Now Kathie asks Forrest who he wants to take him to school and he chooses her, which is fine with me. That means I get to stay with Theo while Kathie takes Forrest to Assembly. His whole school gathers in the gymnasium for Assembly twenty minutes before the school day begins. It really is a nice gathering. They have class theme skits, show-and-tell, songs of all sorts, but mostly patriotic songs. And then there is the salute to the flag of the United States of America. Sag Harbor has more American flags flying. When I first went there I thought it was a national holiday, until I saw them every day. Now I've come to love our flag. It is, I think, the most beautiful of all the flags of the world.

Friday Assemblys are the best time for both Kathie and me to go, and Theo of course. On Fridays all the children link arms and sway together as they sing the Sag Harbor Elementary School Song. The first time I witnessed this, I cried.

So off Kathie and Forrest go, while I stay home with Theo and start to clean up the wreckage as I try to grab a bite to eat at the same time. Theo is squirming in my arms and I'm having trouble getting him back into his high chair. He's such a squirmer. I feel that I can feel him growing in my arms. At last I occupy him with his little plastic melody train with its sounds of barnyard animals and familiar children's tunes mixed together. He seems to be stuck on a duck quacking combined with the melody of "Red River Valley."

Freed up from Theo, I go in to clear the dining-room table of Marissa's mostly uneaten bowl of instant oatmeal and her balled-up, discarded snot rags. I can't stand seeing all the food the kids waste. It drives me wild. I put on ten pounds just eating leftovers and lost maybe three pounds getting under the table at restaurants to pick up piles of dropped pasta, rice, and French fries. I feel so sorry for the busboys. I tip well, but I don't want to feel I have to overtip. I'd rather work it out in trade.

My mom was the same. I remember that she had a little triangular plastic strainer in the corner of the sink where we were supposed to scrape our plates. As soon as we scraped our plates into the strainer, she'd pick out little pieces of food and pop them into her mouth while she admonished us. "Oh, think of the starving Koreans," she'd say. Now, fifty years later, the Koreans are still starving and we are still getting fat eating for them. Theo is a real handful, I think, and then I have a paranoid flash. I think, that's why the federal government encourages large families—once you have one child, you're too busy to even look out the window. Conspiracies could abound, they could be building a nuclear power plant in your back yard and you'd never notice.

When Kathie returns from taking Forrest to school, Theo kicks and flails at the sight of her like a battery-operated child. Kathie lifts Theo out of his high chair and takes him upstairs to her office, where she will try to get some work done. Kathie runs a talent agency out of the house, and with her partner, out of an office in New York City. I was afraid she wouldn't be able to work four days a week at home, but she's found a way to do it.

Downstairs, I at last sit down for some coffee and a look at the morning paper, which has been scattered and wildly disassembled in Marissa's search for information on Spice Girls. At any rate, I'm not really interested in the headlines. I'm looking at one of my favorite sections, the science section.

Then, just as I get the paper assembled in an order to read it, I hear someone knocking on the kitchen door and I see from where I am sitting that it's one of the contractors Kathie has called—to do what, I'm not sure. Maybe he's here to check on the rotting sills under the French doors or give an estimate on Marissa's new bedroom. At any rate, Kathie makes all the calls and has all the dealings with him. Kathie and I aren't married, so she goes by her family name, Russo, and I figure that's good, because so many of the contractors are of Italian-American descent. I figure they'll respond quicker to a Russo than they would to a Gray. Because the house was built in 1890, Kathie is always having to call for help. It needs constant repair. I'm good for none of that. I'm allergic to hammers. All I can do is go out on the road and tell stories about the collapsing house and then bring the money I earn back to pay the repairman.

These contractors, electricians, painters, hedge trimmers, masons always seem to show up in the morning when Kathie is busy up in her office, so I get to greet them. I go to the door in my yoga outfit, which is a combination of baggy gray long johns and a faded red sweatshirt. I mean, I look like a dressed-down Ozzie Nelson who is always on the verge of going to work.

All these service people who come to the door are always a little taken aback by me. They give me the once-over and then say, "Good day. You must be Mister Russo." I've decided it's simpler to answer, "Yes. That's right. I am." So Mister Russo has become my new persona in Sag Harbor, me, Ozzie Russo.

On this particular October day, this contractor has come to speak to Kathie about repairing the rotting sills beneath the French doors. A major job to be done. I call Kathie down from her office and let her take care of it while I at last get to read the paper. I am in search of stories that will lift my anxiety out of myself and relocate it in the world out there.

Oh boy, here's one. Look at this.

UNPREDICTABLE ROGUE ASTEROIDS
Just last year a previously unknown asteroid about the size of Yankee Stadium was spotted only four days before it whipped by the Earth.

That's a good one. Oh, look at this.

WHY MILLSTONE REACTOR WORRIES ME
They have reopened the nuclear reactor in Waterford, Connecticut. With an accidental release of radioactive material, the prevailing northwest wind could carry a radioactive plume over the north and south forks of Long Island, causing an environmental catastrophe that could never be recovered from. An estimated 23,000 dead.

Then it goes on to talk about how there's no evacuation route planned for eastern Long Island, and I think, evacuation route? How can you ever evacuate anyone on the Long Island Expressway?

My God, look at this one in the science section of the paper.

STUDIES SHOW BICYCLE SEATS CAUSE IMPOTENCE
Studies show that bicycle seats compress the main arteries that run under the scrotum and feed the penis erectus.

But why, after all these years of bike riding, has this not been reported before? Then I read further.

Studies show this may have to do with the fact that more older adults are riding bicycles now.

Oh my God, I think, I'm an older adult and I've just bought a bicycle. I do that six-mile loop on my Trek bike every day. That's what keeps me sane. I can't imagine giving up bike riding.

A combination of these stories and four cups of coffee has left me horny. I've got that lower-spinal-chord itch. I can't contain myself and I call up to Kathie, "Kathie . . . Honey, do you want to take a break?"—which is, of course, a euphemism for "do you want to have a quickie?" Before, when Forrest was young, our cue was, "Forrest, do you want to see a Barney video?"

I never dreamed I'd see the day when I could get turned on by a purple dinosaur with cellulite. I mean, that Barney music was like an aphrodisiac for Kathie and me. We'd just hear the opening notes and get hot. Now, with Theo, who is not into videos yet, it takes so little to keep him occupied. All it takes is a brown paper bag filled with some Ban roll-on, a hairbrush, and an unopened bottle of Vitamin C and he's happy. Also, our bed is high enough so that, if we put him on the floor, he can't see us. We do that. We put Theo on the floor to the side of the bed and, tearing our clothes off, we hop in, tangle and quickly fall into making the beast with two backs. While lovemaking, I am careful not to look out the north window at the head of the bed because of that pristine village view of the Baptist church and those white picket fences. If I really get into it, and start to worry about premature ejaculation without satisfying Kathie, I will certainly look out the window at the historic cemetery. That's my graveyard meditation. That really does the trick. Also, it is so strange to be making love in the daylight. My bedroom in my New York City loft had no windows in it, so it acted for years as a perfect out-of-time fantasy sex cave.

Now, just as Kathie and I are getting into it, something happens that completely throws me. I hear this crazy cackling laughter coming out seemingly from between Kathie's legs. Then the laughter turns into a voice and cries, "Help! Stop! That tickles! Stop tickling me!" I jump back and look down under the covers and find a Tickle Me Elmo doll buried in the blankets. Marissa or Forrest or both of them must have left it, or planted it, and Kathie is now laughing. Oh, she is laughing so hard. Even baby Theo is laughing down on the floor. I am not laughing. I can't seem to laugh and maintain an erection at the same time.

Then the laughter subsides and I toss Elmo down to Theo and we get back into the hunky-doryness of it all, and no sooner do we get into it and are rolling than we hear a male voice from down in the kitchen yell, "Electrician!" Kathie moans and says, "Oh no, the electrician has come to rewire the attic for Marissa's room." Kathie jumps up and puts on her bathrobe, at the same time scooping Theo up off the floor. She calls to the electrician, "I'll be right down." Then to me she turns and says, "We'll do it later in your writer's studio when Theo's asleep." Yeah, I bet, I think. There'll never be time for it. And I go into the bathroom to splash cold water on my gennies and get ready for my bike ride.

I dress for my bike ride the same way I dressed when I was a ten-year-old and rode my Schwinn to school. I'm far from a spandexed Day-Glo gear-head. I really dress down, with my corduroys' right leg stuffed into my sock and an elastic band to hold my pant leg in and away from the bike chain. I put on a sweatshirt, a windbreaker, and I'm ready to take off. Then, just as I'm about to go out the door, Kathie catches me in the kitchen and asks me to take Theo just for a moment while she goes upstairs to show the electrician the attic.

Once again, Theo is squirming in my arms and I don't know how to calm him. I don't remember Forrest being as active as this guy is. Had he been, I don't know if I would have bonded with him as quickly and as easily as I did. Then, standing there in the kitchen, with struggling Theo in my arms, I remember what it is I have to do to calm him down. All I have to do is walk outside with him. He's my outdoor boy born in that storm, pulled into the world at the tail end of a nor'easter, he's my outdoor bliss kid. I just step out the door of the kitchen and into the yard and hold him with my arms under his legs and his back to my chest and I aim him out as if he were my camera. I look down at his head as though I am looking down into a view finder, as though I am looking out through his eyes. I stand still and feel him give off a little shudder as he enters into what I can only call an "awe-some state." He is in a pure state of fearful awe, as if he sees something I don't see. It's as if he perceives the landscape in 1660, pre-settled and wild. Then he shifts into his bliss state and begins to let out little Ooh's and Ahh's followed by that little old Italian winemaker chuckle as he takes it all in and seems to delight in all he sees. He is my new bliss-eyes as I aim him toward the west to see the wooden fence all covered with English ivy. Then I tilt him up a little bit to see the broad yellowing leaves of the mulberry trees that run along the back side of the fence. Now, as I pan Theo from west to north, we sweep past the corner of Robert Lowell and Caroline Black-wood's last home. Through the autumn foliage we catch only a little corner of it, which looks like a giant piece of wedding cake. Then I pan Theo past my writer's shed, which has become more like a storage closet and a secret sex pad than it has a place for writing. We at last come to the garden, and the north fence, against which two beautiful end-of-the-season red roses grow. Seeing the roses, Theo lets out another little cooing "Oooh," and then that laugh again. That little old Italian winemaker laugh again. Above the north fence, we see the gabled peaks of the modest home of our next-door neighbors, Carlos and Marie. They are an older couple, perhaps in their early seventies, and are semiretired. Carlos is originally from Peru and Marie is from Australia, so they make for a dynamic duo. They are young at heart and very spontaneous together. Once, I ran into them on my way to go sailing in my little day-sailer and asked them if they wanted to come along with me. It was such a wild and windy day that I wasn't even sure if I should go out at all. Anyway, I just half jokingly invited them for a sail, and to my surprise, they said, "Yes." We all went sailing together and all got quite wet. We also all got a little frightened together. Carlos and Marie are sometimes like two old teenagers and they love our children, so we have them over quite often, or they invite us to their house. They are really like grandparents to our children.

I am only a little nervous when Carlos first sees me and tries to back me into a corner with his latest jokes. I'm really not one for long, complicated jokes. They often feel like long, seventh-grade math problems, where I am afraid of missing one of the elements and then not getting it, not being able to laugh, and end up having to fake it. One of his jokes, though, I shall never forget. It's so simple and short. It's like a visual haiku and it goes like this: "A skeleton walks into a bar and orders a glass of beer and a mop."

For all sorts of reasons, I liked that joke a lot. I liked it so much that I even worked it into a monologue that I was performing which was based on my life in Sag Harbor. Then a funny thing happened. I invited Marie and Carlos to see the monologue, and after they saw it, Carlos gave up telling jokes. It was as though he didn't want to be remembered for just telling jokes. He got more serious with me and even started quoting poetry to me. Then one day when he was visiting us with Marie, he said, "I have discovered such a good lyric right there in downtown Sag Harbor. It was hanging in the window of that store named *Our Gig Two, whatever*. It was hanging right next to that little plaque that reads, ON THIS SITE IN 1897 NOTHING HAPPENED. It was an old Grateful Dead lyric by Robert Hunter." Then Carlos switched into this supercharged and very intense theatrical mode and quoted the lines as if reciting Walt Whitman:

> *Sometimes the light's all shining on me*
> *Other times I can barely see*
> *Lately it occurs to me*
> *What a long, strange trip it's been.*

Much as I love that quote, it worried me that Carlos might be losing his sense of humor, seeing as he never told me jokes anymore, and it was funny, because I sort of missed them. Even though I never remembered his jokes, I missed seeing, and feeling, the pleasure Carlos took in telling them. In fact, I even began to pay attention to jokes that I heard elsewhere in hopes that I might remember one to tell Carlos, and that did, at last, happen. One night, just as Kathie and I were taking the children home after yet another super meal at Carlos and Marie's, I turned to Carlos and said: "A drunk walks into a bar and yells, 'All lawyers are assholes!' And this guy jumps up and yells, 'Watch it, mister!' The drunk says, 'What? Are you a lawyer?' 'No,' he says. 'I'm an asshole.' "

It was as though I had drawn a gun in a quick-draw shoot-out. Carlos doubled over as though he'd been shot. He just doubled over with laughter and gasps of "yes yes yes!"

Now I turn Theo to the east and see privet hedge, trees, crisscrossing of phone wires, and that white church steeple again, which rises into the clear blue autumn sky like a transcendent note of concretized pure white music. And on the gold cross reflecting the sun, a seagull sits. It's just perched and sitting there so very still, like a weather-vane reproduction of itself.

Then, for our last turn, Theo and I look south at the house. My first real home for me in my adult life. It is a simple straight up-and-down green clapboard wooden Victorian house. Also, because of the French doors that cover the first floor ends of the house, it looks a little like a dollhouse: it is open, as though waiting for some big giant's hand to reach in and move the furniture around or pluck one of the children out. Sometimes, on windy autumn nights, I will sneak out into the yard so I can peek in on my dollhouse family and see, there in the living room, the children playing in front of the roaring fire. Then, on the other side of the wall, not seen by them, I see, through the kitchen French doors, Kathie, the mother, in the kitchen. There she is, doing her cooking and cleaning and cleaning and cooking.

Kathie and the electrician come down from the attic and I hand Theo back to Kathie and get my Trek bike out of the writer's studio. Then, just to make sure that I am all emptied out for my ride, I go to my little corner where the privet hedge meets the west wall, all covered with English ivy, and there I take a quick pee while looking up at one lone gull soaring overhead. And I think as I pee, I would never want to own a house with a yard not private enough to pee in without being seen. Finishing up, I walk my bike out through our little white gate and at last, I am off. As soon as I get out on the road I start to unwind and I start thinking. "Wow, why has it taken me so long to get out of there?" Now I'm riding past the historic cemetery on my left, to turn right on Jermain Avenue and ride by the other, not quite so historic cemetery, Oakland Cemetery. How I love these cemeteries. They are such great negative spaces and it's nice to be almost sure that the greedy contractors can't develop there. Now I am riding past the duck pond on my right and headed for the intersection of Main Street and Brick Kiln Road. I ride straight through the traffic light, which takes me very quickly out of the historic village of Sag Harbor and into a hodgepodge of crazy, mixed-up architecture. I pass the fire station on my right, which gives me a clear view of my first American flag of the day, which tells me in its colorful way that we have a healthy northwest wind (I remember the prevailing wind that brings our daily radioactive dose over from the Millstone Reactor) blowing at about fifteen knots. So that means as I turn right on Noyac Road I will be heading into the wind and will have to push a little harder. I like that. I like having to do that because riding harder is both waking me up and focusing me in a good way as I ride with my own self-imposed invisible blinders on. I am being careful not to look at or take in too much of this geography of nowhere, or anywhere. It could be anywhere in central Long Island. It could be Huntington, Amityville, or Syosset. It's all an homogeny of random, chaotic styles. There are row houses, ranch houses, split-levels with fake brass carriage lamps mounted by the door. Beach bungalows, one two-day-old prefab I'd not noticed before. And then there are the great, three-million-dollar baronic trophy homes with four oversized faux Provence château-style chimneys and a four-car garage, just plunked down there in the middle of an unlandscaped potato field. These houses are used only three months of the year. I also see vinyl-sided colonial-style houses with oversized large-load white plastic shrink-wrapped power boats looking like giant Clorox bottles perched on undersized trailers in the yard. I see Boston whalers and rusting Buicks for sale, jeeps for sale, night crawlers, firewood, pick-your-own-pumpkins-here, hot rods, speedboats, lobster pots, live bait and snails. Oh, the stupefying clutter of it all!

Then, all of a sudden, "POW!" I'm out and riding along the water and shock-a-roo! It's a million-dollar view! It's all a glorious out-of-season Caribbean blue! Now that northwest wind is behind me and driving me on as my head opens up over the bay. Seagulls hover and soar and that old familiar smell of autumn mixed with brine enters and fills me. I am riding fast and smooth now with the brilliant energizing bay on my left, then out of the Long Beach parking lot, I ride onto Route 114. And coming in for my final run as I pass the North Haven Settlement sign which reads "Settled in 1664," I turn right at the blinking light, I turn right and head for my final run to the little bridge that goes over the estuary to Sag Harbor Cove and links North Haven to the village of Sag Harbor. As I ride now I see roadkill. Dead squirrels smashed on the road. And I smell the reek of a dead deer on the side. I spy the gaping torn anus where the first little critters have gnawed their hungry way in. Then I see that angering pile of discarded 7-Eleven coffee cups that keeps growing in the same place every day, because the same workers just happen to finish their coffee at that spot as they turn in to build yet another giant trophy home.

Then suddenly I feel that tingle in my crotch. I realize my whole crotch has gone to sleep. I've lost all the feeling in my groin, so I jump off my bike and walk it for a while. As I walk, I enjoy the feeling of the blood rushing back in.

Now for the final homestretch I ride up onto the bridge that spans the channel of water that separates Sag Harbor from North Haven. When I get to the center of the bridge I stop. There in the middle of the bridge I am up high enough to have my first partial overview of the town. Just to my left I see a sweet little cove that may soon be destroyed by Tommy Mottola, the president of Sony Music, who is trying to build a two-hundred-foot-long private jet-ski dock. I try to block this great giant penis party dock out of my mind and enjoy what's left of the pristine cove for what it is now. Beyond this cove I see the long wharf, where the whaling ships used to come in. I see another American flag blowing maybe twenty knots now and I see the harbor with its elegant sailboats. Then I see the breakwater and the bay beyond. In the distance, I see the nature conservancy on Shelter Island. It's so lovely to see such undeveloped land all stretching out in that autumnal, purplish rusty hue.

To my right I see what looks like a sort of medieval wall of a motel, condos, two professional buildings, and three restaurants, all surrounding the village, which peaks up behind them like a pop-up card with old colonial brick-and-clapboard Victorians, and all its churches. Then, in its ludicrous way, as if put there to save the town from becoming a piece of generic calendar art, there sits a big blue one-hundred-foot-high natural-gas ball. It looks like a giant pool ball that has just rolled into town and come to rest.

I love this little overview and I think, as I stand on that bridge, I wish the town had a little hill I could climb up and look back down from. I would love to climb up a hill just to get that godly distance on it all, just to have that overview. Once, I did have a God's-eye overview, when I was flying back from London with my family in a giant 747. We flew right over Sag Harbor in the daylight and we all looked down at the old Whalers' Church, at our house and the long wharf. It was a true God's-eye view and all of Sag Harbor looked like a Norman Rockwell Monopoly town. It was all just nestled there with its off-season population of 2,009, about the size of the population of an average New York City subway at rush hour.

I remember the first time I rode over this bridge on my new bike just after moving here. I remember the feeling of what I can only call a complicated present. By that I mean where I am present and in the past at the same time. It was because the place was so familiar in a very old sense and yet, at the same time, new. I felt as though I'd come home to Rhode Island without quite having to go there. Rhode Island is, as the gull flies, only about thirty miles northeast. Standing there on that bridge for the first time, I felt as if I had returned to the place that I started from and was about to know it for the first time. Circles are, I think, so important to me, or to us. Circles are important because we only live once. Repeating, or coming around full circle, gives us the feeling of rebirth, of living again. The seasons do that as well. These circles bend the relentless, unmarked horizontal march of time. They take us away and they bring us back. So, after thirty years of self-imposed exile from my land of islands and sea, I came full circle, and as I stood there on that bridge the idea occurs to me that if I wrapped my arms around myself, and just stood there so very, very still, I would feel that I had at last come home. I felt that if I stood very still I would finally feel a sense of belonging. I would feel connected to this place, this single place on Earth.

I stood there for the longest time, just waiting. I stood and I waited. I stood, but I never felt the stillness I was longing for. All I felt was motion all around and under me. Like the water flowing under that very bridge. The stillness never came, but what did come was the realization that there is no place where we can arrive. It is all transiency, impermanence, and change. When I realized this, I felt the only appropriate thing to do was be in motion, so I got on my bike and I rode.

The noon whistle breaks my reverie and brings me back to the warm immediacy of this lunch hour. What a cozy set of words, *lunch hour*. This is when all the workers all over town lay their burdens down and open up their plain brown sandwich bags, or go home for homemade chowder, or stop at the IGA on Main Street in town, which is where I'm headed. I love that little IGA on Main Street because it's like a play store. It's the kind of store we created as kids with just enough items, just one of some things. There is no overload or plethora of product, there are just simple bare essentials. It's like shopping in Eastern Europe.

When I hear the noon whistle, I ride down and go to the IGA and stand in the deli line with the other workers. I stand there, me, Ozzie Russo, ordering ham salad, a hard roll, and a can of Campbell's tomato soup, which I will bring home to share with Theo and Kathie at our round table in the dining room. It's noon, October 8, 1997.

After lunch I think, what shall I do? What can I do? I feel like I have to lay my hands on something. I've got to do some work with my hands. Then I think, oh yes, of course, I'll get out the lawnmower. That's something I can do. The lawn could use one last cut for the season. I go to get the hand mower out of the toolshed. I bought a hand mower as soon as we moved to Sag Harbor because we had one when I was a kid and I love the crisp, metallic sound of it cutting. Also, our lawn in Sag Harbor is small enough to cut with a hand mower, so why bother buying a power mower? I hate the sound of motors. As a kid I cut my lawn with a hand mower, but as a young adult I became less and less interested in what I'd come to experience as "the real world." I sort of started to distrust hand mowers and real people. People were imperfect and rarely dramatic enough for me, and a real hand mower always got dull, would rust or break. Also, I wasn't real interested in replicating the traditional family structure I'd grown up in. I was not interested in creating my own American nuclear family. So, instead of entering into a relationship with the so-called real world, I ran off and joined an experimental theatre company where we created our own worlds. I think this theatre company was also a substitute for a more traditional family. One of the things we did was to take famous plays and deconstruct them to fit our sensibilities. One of the plays we deconstructed was Eugene O'Neill's *Long Day's Journey into Night*. Before joining the experimental theatre company, when I was a more traditional actor but still in search of the Land of Let's Pretend, I acted in a more traditional production of *Long Day's Journey into Night* and I remember the full-length version of that play runs for about four hours. For our production, I just took the text of the play and underlined all my favorite lines I remembered from the previous production I was in. Then we abstracted those lines, which reduced the play to seven minutes. We developed a highly choreographed production with a fog machine and crazy lights all done to Berlioz's *Roman Carnival Overture*, which, coincidentally, also runs for seven minutes. It was a beautiful production. Willem Dafoe was dressed as a woman, to play Mary Tyrone, the mother. I played the role of James Tyrone, the father. For me, there was one very beautiful moment that Elizabeth LeCompte, the director, choreographed for me. She choreographed a wild dance with a yellow hand mower, and I eventually did that dance so many times in rehearsal and in the run of the show that that lawn mower was transformed from a lawn mower into an object of art. After our production of *Long Day's Journey into Night*, I never experienced a hand mower in the same way again.

Standing now with my hand mower in the back yard of my Sag Harbor home, I feel, not that I am about to cut the lawn, but rather that I am in a play directed by who I'm not sure. It's as if I'm on a stage, or a movie set, waiting for the action to begin. I feel like Ozzie Russo, who is being played by Spalding Gray, who is playing at being a family man here in the Let's Pretend yard of life. Then I just jump into it. I enter and begin the scene of cutting the lawn.

Just after doing a pleasurable few passes with the mower, I notice Kathie, out of the corner of my good eye, barefoot, dressed in jeans and a bra, slinking toward my writer's studio. And I think, Oh I love this woman. She's such an initiator. She's such a phallic lady. I stop, turn, and look at her, and standing there, I suddenly become "the gardener."

We meet at the doorway of my writer's studio and pass in without speaking and there, among the clutter of garbage bags filled with mothballs and winter clothes, bicycles, and Theo's giant 1948 gray perambulator, and the sounds of Carlos puttering in his driveway just behind the studio, we hold each other so very tight and then complete ourselves on the edge of my writer's table.

After I finish cutting the lawn I wonder if I have time for a quick sail in my little beetle boat, but then, when I check the time, I am both pleased and surprised to see it is already two-thirty in the afternoon. Great! Time for me to pick Forrest up at school. (Oh, Forrest, save me from the void.) I have something so very meaningful to do. I will go pick him up from school and take him downtown to rent a video. We don't have a television in our home. We just have a playback monitor for the VCR. Kathie and I have been real committed to keeping TV out of our house. When we moved there we just didn't buy one, and for all of us, it has made a great difference. Also, I had a chance to see what uncontrolled TV watching could do to Forrest last summer. We had rented a house for the month of August in Martha's Vineyard and there was cable television there. Forrest would get up, turn it on, and watch about three or four hours straight, only to stop when we shut the television down to go to the beach. This shutting down of the TV would cause Forrest to go into what looked like heavy withdrawal symptoms, like a heroin addict coming off the needle. He would bang his head on the couch and wail, "What am I going to do?" And I'd say, "But, Forrest, we're going to the ocean to play in the waves." And he would cry back at me, "But think of all the shows I'll be missing while we're there."

On my way to pick Forrest up at kindergarten, I think about last year, when I would pick him up at his pre-school. I think about the way he would, as soon as he saw me, streak across the lawn, crying, "Daddy!" Then he'd jump into my arms and I'd spin him around. I thought that would go on for years, or at least five years. But in kindergarten they march Forrest out with all the other children and line them up along a hurricane fence, like a police lineup, for the parents to come and identify them. Now that he doesn't dash out to me, I have a hard time recognizing him at first. Today, when I spot him, I get real excited and yell, "Hi honey!" Then, as soon as I hear myself, I get real self-conscious and think, Oh my God, is it still all right to call him "honey" in public? I mean, he is five years old and all the other fathers are there with their sons saying, "Hi guy! Yo sport. Hey fella'! Let's get cracking! Awesome. Yeah, we're outta' here. Whatever."

I say softly as he walks beside me now, "Hi honey. Did you have a good day at school? We're going to go get your bike and take a ride downtown to rent a video this afternoon." We're out of the schoolyard and on the road now. And it's about this point on the walk home when Forrest begins his litany of etymological-derivation questions, and he starts right in on me with, "Dad, could I tell you something? Why do they call a road a road?" I usually tell him, as I do today, "Forrest, you know I don't know a whole lot about where words come from. I'm still trying to figure that out for myself." But Forrest continues on with his, "Dad, could I tell you something? How do cars come into the world?" Suddenly I see an old black-and-white seventh-grade science film from my past, narrated by Ed Herlihy. I see a big, what I think is a big, Bessemer furnace pouring what? Is it iron or steel? They call it "Iron City," don't they? Or is it "Steel Town"? And what's the difference between iron and steel, I wonder. And what about metal? What the hell is metal? It's certainly not Metal Town. They never called it Metal Town. Then I see a conveyor belt or assembly line filled with half-built bodies of 1949 Fords. Looking over to Forrest, I also see that he's already well onto his next thought. "Dad, could I tell you something? I think I know why they call a fish a fish."

"Really, honey? Tell me why."

"Because it has a fin and that begins with the sound 'ph.' Dad, I know why they call a hotel a hotel."

"Well, why, Forrest?"

"It's because when the whole family gets to the hotel they all start laughing. They laugh 'ho ho ho ho ho' and then they 'tell,' Dad. They tell all about what happened on their way there. Get it, Dad? Ho-tell."

At home, Forrest puts his big purple crash helmet on,

which makes him look like a purple cockroach. Then we get his bike with the trainer wheels on it out of my writer's shed and we are off for the Long Wharf Video store. The store is just at the bottom of Main Street out on the wharf. It's not more than six or seven blocks away, but I know it will be a long trip, because Forrest cannot ride his bike and ask questions at the same time. And he loves to ask questions.

Just outside our gate, he rides for a bit and then brakes and turns to me to say, "Dad, could I tell you something? Aliens don't have armpits."

"How do you know?"

"I just do, Dad."

"Dad, could I tell you something? I know what's inside ghosts."

"Oh, really, Forrest? Well then, what is inside ghosts?"

"Nothing, Dad."

"And what is nothing, Forrest?"

"Nothing is just a word, Dad. But, Dad, 'oh my' is not a bad word, is it?"

"No, Forrest, I've told you over and over there are no bad words. A word only starts to take on a good or bad meaning when it's used in context, and we'll discuss that one later. Also, 'oh' and 'my' are two words, not one."

"But my teacher said we could not say 'Oh my God.' "

"Forrest, you can say any word you want. You can say 'God.' You can say 'my.' You can say 'oh.' You can say 'God my oh.' Now let's go over the lesson again. What might your teacher think is a real bad word? Let's take a good bad word. Now there's a concept, a 'good' bad word. Let's take 'shit.' Well now, we don't have the word 'shit' yet, do we, so we're going to have to construct it. Create it. Now I'm going to write the word 'shit' in the air. It starts with the letter 's.' Now is 's' a bad letter? Does it smell? No. My first name begins with 's.' It's kind of a nice snaky letter. Now we make the 'h.' Anything bad about that? No. Now we have 'i' and now 't.' There it is, Forrest, there's the word, 's-h-i-t,' written in the air. Now please don't mistake the word with the substance in the toilet. The substance in the toilet is the-thing-in-itself. It smells and it has some offensive properties. Don't confuse the word with the substance. The word is only a signifier. Now, Forrest, the Bible had it somewhat wrong, or at least the Book of John did. The Book of John says, 'In the beginning was the word.' The opening of Genesis is more right on. It says, 'In the beginning God created . . .' Now you can forget about God for the time being and just think of the act of creation. That's all verb. That's all action. So we have 'the act,' the creation, and then we have the substance created. That's what we call the-thing-in-and-for-itself, and then we have the name. You see, only after it's something does it get named. Now look, wait, I've got another idea. Let's try writing the word 'shit' with a stick here in the dirt. Will writing it in the dirt make it a dirty word? No, because we have to carve the dirt out with a stick in order to make the word. So it really is an absence of dirt, isn't it?"

I put the stick down and look up at Forrest and realize that I've gone a little bit too far with the lesson this time. Forrest looks up at me and says, "Are you all right, Dad?"

Next we stop at the bank to get some cash from the ATM. Forrest has no interest in coming into the bank with me, although it's not really the bank I'm going into, it's the entrance to the bank, where the ATM is. Forrest waits outside, and as I go in, a little phrase passes in my head, like a song: "Where have all the tellers gone?/ Long time passing." And at that moment I realize I have never seen the inside of my local bank. I was late to get an ATM card. I might never have come to have one if my accountant hadn't arranged it for me, and I remember now, like it was the olden days, walking into my New York City bank. I remember feeling the grand open space of it and seeing the guards and the vaults filled with real money. I remember seeing the smiley bank officers at their open, unpartitioned desks. All these officers smiling and saying, "Good morning, Mr. Gray." Then there was the line of customers waiting for the tellers. Some of those female tellers were so sexy, and cute, and the almost automatic way they counted the money made them even cuter and sexier. I often thought of their underwear and how and where it fit them, rather than the new crisp bills they counted out for me. There was a whole world there, now gone, that Forrest will never see. What a ludicrous idea that it would come to this, sticking a card in one metallic crack and watching crisp, fresh twenties come out of another. And I do it. I stick my card in and watch the money come out. Then, like the old days, not trusting a machine any more than I trust a teller, I go into the corner and count my twenties to check for any mistakes. It always takes at least a couple of counts, because I am the one who's always counting wrong, not the machine. Loving the feel of that little bundle of cash, I stick it deep into my pocket, where it rests next to that other warm bundle. I love the feel of that paper money and I have no real interest in plastic. I prefer paper to plastic any day.

Outside, Forrest is sitting on his bike waiting for me and ready with, "Dad, why do they call a bank a bank?"

"Well now, let me see . . ." I say. "Maybe it has to do with 'embankment,' like money in, water out." Then I think, but why is a riverbank called a riverbank? Forrest is already way down the sidewalk in his little bike, giving peace signs to passersby. These peace signs are new for him. He learned how to make a peace sign from his baby-sitter, Theresa, who has been for us . . . I almost said "a godsend," and I guess I could say that. She answered an ad that Kathie put in the local paper and now we don't know how we can function as a family without her. She served in the Merchant Marines for six years and is pretty good at fixing just about everything, from drafty windows to computers. She has a three-year-old daughter named Ciena who comes with her and then becomes a new part of our family, particularly when they have sleepovers. Theresa has taught Forrest how to make a peace sign and he is doing it to everyone he sees on the street. It's fun for me to step back and watch the reaction of some of the people, some returning it, some pretending they don't see it.

Just before we reach the five-and-dime store, there is a little bench where Mary, our one homeless person in town, always sits. There she sits, toothless, holding a cup of coffee and smoking a cigarette. As soon as she spots you she chokes out, "Dollar? Got a dollar for me?" If I have a dollar, I give it to her, and I do today, but today I stop briefly to engage her in conversation. "What's up?" I ask, and Mary replies, "What's up? Well, it's an important day." "Why?" I ask, and she says, "Because today I have lunch with the Mayor to talk about at last letting all the dead out of that cemetery. They've been in there long enough, don't you think? It's time they went home." "Good luck with your project," I say as I follow Forrest toward the five-and-dime.

The five-and-dime has to be a foreign concept to Forrest—that something, one day, could actually have been bought for a nickel or a dime. Looking down at him stop there, I assume that he wants to go in. I assume that he wants something, and I ask him, "Forrest, do you want to go in?" He answers with that little adult phrase of speech, that little chipper, uptone you might hear someone use at a cocktail party when they are trying not to drink too much and they are just offered another drink, and they say, "No thanks. I'm fine."

I love how Forrest is not a great or grand aquisitor. I love the way he's able to let things go in a generous way. I fell in love with him when he was only two and he would let his balloons go. He would get all excited when he first got the balloon and then, after playing with it for a while, he'd just let it go and watch it drift up into the clouds and disappear forever. I fell in love with him when we were making cupcakes in Martha's Vineyard, and before he made one for himself, he made one for his sister, who was staying with her father for the month of August. Then, after making it, he kept it for her until September. I fell in love with him again on that first Halloween in Sag Harbor. Forrest and Marissa had been downtown getting candy from all the shops, and Marissa wanted to go uptown to all the *big* houses, but Forrest didn't want to go. He wanted to go home with me because he said he had "had enough." Enough candy! Kathie took Marissa to the big houses to trick-or-treat while I took Forrest home.

When we got home, Forrest started giving away his candy to the children when they came to the door, because we had run out of candy, and when they no longer came to the door, he went out in the streets looking for them.

I turn to him once more and say, "Are you sure you don't want something in the five-and-dime?" To which he replies once more, "No, thanks, Dad. I'm fine."

The Sag Harbor five-and-dime is such a gem. It can't have changed much since it was built in 1922. It reminds me of the one in Warren, Rhode Island, our dad used to take us to every Saturday when he would give us each a dime to buy anything we wanted, which would always be a World War II tin soldier or a statue of Ike or maybe Douglas MacArthur with his sunglasses and corncob pipe. Although I remember those plaster replicas as something very special that might have cost more like fifty or seventy-five cents. Then I remember, and I tell Forrest, the story of my Grandfather Gray. I tell him about the time he took me to the Warren five-and-dime and said, "Spuddy boy, buy anything you want in this whole store. It's on me." I didn't know what to make of this. I hardly knew what to make of my Grandfather Gray, because he'd basically not been in my life. When my Grandmother Gray divorced him early on in their marriage, he would have nothing to do with her or my father for years, until he got his own family, and I wonder now as I stand there in front of this five-and-dime with my son how my Grandfather Gray could have neglected his son like that. I mean, not to even have written his son a letter? This is a hard thought, as a father, for me to process. It seems more incomprehensible now than ever before. As for my Grandmother Gray, she was a courageous, strong, single parent. She started her own dress shop in Brookline, Massachusetts, and raised my father on her own. She even sent him to Brown University during the Depression. Because of what little I came to know of my Grandfather Gray, whose birthday I was born on, I came to appreciate how hard it was sometimes for Dad to be a dad. He did not have any role model to work from. He had really grown up without a father.

"So, Forrest," I tell him now, "when I was about your age, or maybe a year older, my Grandfather Gray took me into the Warren five-and-dime and said, 'Spuddy boy [Forrest lets out a big laugh at hearing his dad called 'Spuddy boy.' He laughs and then repeats it out loud], buy anything you want in this store.'"

"What did you do, Dad?" Forrest asks, looking up in suspense.

"Well, I was so overwhelmed by that dizzy feeling that comes from so many possibilities that I just grabbed the first thing I saw. I grabbed a little whisk broom from the home-services department."

"And what did your grandfather say, Dad?"

"He got real stern with me and said, 'No, Spuddy boy. You didn't hear me, I said anything you want in this whole store.' I said, 'But I want this.' And he bought that little whisk broom for me."

Now we pass the real estate windows filled with pictures of houses for sale. There are more real estate offices than there are churches in Sag Harbor. We walk past the liquor store and the IGA. Forrest must be satisfied for a while by that story I told him. I have a chance to look around, and as I look around at the few people on the street, I marvel how my eye is not caught and instantly drawn to some sexy woman. What a change from New York City, where the women wear their sexuality upon their sleeves. After growing up enough finally to realize I could never directly experience even a little portion of what I saw on the streets of New York, I got tired of seeing it. I became a drooling vicarian with a big fantasy head. That constant flow of apparently available flesh on the streets undermined my attempted choice of being with just one woman. It just wore me out. It became for me a nervous distraction like what I used to feel when I went to the dollar-ninety-nine-cent porn movies on Eighth Avenue. They were an inspiration for masturbation and little more. When I got older, and stopped masturbating, I didn't want to go out of my loft, because of what I saw. The streets were adrift with anonymous sexy women like many a man's dream turned to a nightmare. Oh well, I was past all that now, thank God. Now, as I look around me on Main Street, Sag Harbor, I realize I am no longer distracted and I don't miss it. I realize that I'm not shopping anymore. I am monogamous and I have, for better or worse, settled down in this seaside town to live and grow old with my family. This is what I think and as I think it I hope that it is true, will hold, will endure.

Just past the IGA, Forrest stops his bike again and says, "Dad, could I tell you something?"

"Sure, sweetie. What is it?"

"Why are deer poops so small? Because, Dad, a deer is almost as big as a horse and the poops are the size of a rabbit's."

"That's a good question, Forrest," I say. "And as soon as I get home, I am going to look that up in the *Encyclopedia Britannica*. I knew I bought those books from that traveling salesman for a reason."

"Also, Dad, could I tell you one more thing? Why can't we feel the Earth spin?"

"Now, that's another good question, Forrest. Because I know the Earth is spinning right now. I am going to look that one up, too, just as soon as we get home."

Almost to the video store now, Forrest stops to deliver one last bull's-eye of a question.

He says, "Dad, could I tell you something? How do flies celebrate?"

"What?" I say, not sure that I have heard him right. And then he repeats it, "Dad, how do flies celebrate?"

Then, without missing a beat, the answer comes to me

and I simply give it to him, "Well, now, basically I'd have to say by flying from one pile of poop to another."

We both laugh together as we pass by the seventeenth-century stocks, then the eighteenth-century windmill, and walk into the twentieth-century Long Wharf Video store.

Forrest is always pretty set on what he wants to get before we go into the store. Today he is set on *James and the Giant Peach*, and he has recommended to me *The Nutty Professor*. He has already seen *The Nutty Professor* with his mom and his sister, Marissa, and he thinks I'd like it because of all the great fart jokes. So, off he goes to look for *James and the Giant Peach* while I go back to look for *The Nutty Professor*. When I go to the counter with the empty box, the woman proprietor says, looking across the store to Forrest, "Is that your son?" When I say, "Yes," she says, "Oh, not for the boy. Not this movie for the little boy."

I say, "But he has already seen it and he is recommending it to me." At the same time I think, oh no, we are not long for this town after all. I'd had the same reaction just about a year ago before I even found out about the Millstone Reactor reopening, which was to be a good enough reason for fleeing this beautiful town. I'd also thought about fleeing when Kathie told me that she got a call from one of Forrest's pre-school teachers about his ribald outspokenness on a class field trip to Montauk. It seems Forrest was doing some premature sex education with his young male friends. He was telling them, in a loud voice, that he knew how babies were born. He told them that it happened when the penis goes into the "Pagina." After this happened, his teacher called Kathie to tell her what Forrest said and that she felt she was going to have to call the other mothers to warn them about what their children had been exposed to. When Kathie told me this, that is when I started my little litany of "Oh Kathie, we're not long for this town. We're not long for this town."

Now we are all set with *James and the Giant Peach* and *The Nutty Professor*. Going out of the video store, I notice on a novelty shelf a collection of esoteric videos and I am taken back by a video of *The Tibetan Book of the Dead* narrated by Leonard Cohen. The blurb on the box says something like, "See lifelike animated spirits coming out of the recently dead, a must see."

So that decides it. We now have *James and the Giant Peach*, *The Nutty Professor*, and *The Tibetan Book of the Dead*. Three videos that will make for a very eclectic afternoon and evening of viewing.

Outside the video store Forrest insists, as he always does, on looking at and naming the three rented videos. When he gets to *The Tibetan Book of the Dead* he asks me what it's about and I tell him that will take some explaining, which I will do when we get home. To this, Forrest replies, "Oh I get it, Dad. You don't want to spoil it for me."

Instead of heading home, I turn and start to walk out to the end of the long wharf. Forrest follows me. The children don't seem to understand my need for this. Whenever I get close to the water, I need to walk out on the wharf and just look out over the harbor. I always feel my head open up as I look out over the harbor and across the bay to Shelter Island in the distance. I like to stand there and imagine that long wharf in the eighteen-hundreds when whaling ships came in after as much as three years at sea. I like to imagine them unloading their barrels of whale oil. Also, I like to look down to the Sag Harbor yacht yard to see if I can see my little sailboat, my little beetle catboat, my day-sailer named *Small*. What a gem that boat is. It's a little fifteen-foot catboat with wooden spars and gaff rigging. When it's running with a good wind, it looks as if it is sailing out of a Winslow Homer painting.

Oh, I had such fantasies of family sails when we first

moved out to Sag Harbor and Kathie was pregnant with Theo. We had only one sail together where Forrest lay bored on the floor with his eyes closed, sucking on his bottle of apple juice and saying, "When are we going to be home?" Then Marissa, the great drama queen that she was then at only ten, cried out, every time the boat heeled with the wind in the slightest, "Help! Coast guard, coast guard! Help me! I don't want to die a virgin!"

Now I sail alone mostly, or sometimes I take Kathie and Theo for a quick sail because Theo is my outdoor bliss kid and just loves to sail. As for myself, I love to sail alone, to go out on a breezy late-September afternoon with no other boats in sight and just sail around listening to, and feeling, the water and the wind while they take me for a ride.

When we get to the end of the wharf, I take one deep breath and try not to think of the levels of radiation from that nuclear reactor, but I can no longer totally shut it out of my mind. It is our new dark cloud over this sweet town.

I take Forrest's hand and walk him back to his bike, where he begins his ride home past the American Hotel, past the Town Hall, and we stop in front of the toy store.

It is a beautiful and well-stocked toy store. When we first moved to Sag Harbor, Forrest would always want to go in and buy something, but today he just seems satisfied to look in the window, just the way he did at the five-and-dime. "Do you want to go in, Forrest?" I ask, to which he replies, "No, thanks, Dad. I'm fine." I love him too much today. I can't believe how good he's being and also how blessed Kathie and I are to have such a well-balanced child . . . today. I never pay much heed to astrology, but I can't help thinking about Forrest being a Libra and how he just keeps balancing his scales. I don't mean to say he doesn't have his fits and wretched moods, but they can almost always be traced to a lack of sleep. He often stays up too late with his big sister, talking, watching videos, or just lying there with her, listening for ghosts. Now I feel such warmth and good cheer toward Forrest I want to stop at the Harbor Deli to get him a treat, and to my surprise, he orders an Orangina instead of a Coke, because he doesn't want to be hyper. I buy him an Orangina, and a Poland Spring water for myself, and we take them and sit at one of the little tables in the window, where we are surrounded by a group of retired older men sipping coffee and just staring out the window and waiting.

Then Forrest starts in again, "Dad, could I tell you something? What if you were Howard Stern?"

And I say, "Oh, Forrest, that question confounds me. It would be a different world from the one we live in now if I were Howard Stern, and what would it all mean? Would it mean that I would be on the radio looking like him and feeling like me? Would some version of him be sitting here with you? I just don't know how to think about that kind of question, honey."

Then Forrest says, "All I know, Dad, is that Mom wouldn't like it."

"Why not?" I ask.

"Because he's Fartman, Dad," Forrest replies.

And I say, "But your dad is Fartman, too, sometimes, Forrest."

Then Forrest says, "Yeah, but not onstage you're not, Dad."

"Well that's true, sweetie," I say, and then go on to re-mind him about an incident at the Avis car rental in New York City. We were renting a car to go out to Sag Harbor for a final look at the house that we ended up buying. It was a Saturday morning and we were in a real rush. Also, I had started to come down with a cold, so with my breakfast of a spinach-and-feta-cheese omelet, I had eaten a few thousand milligrams of Vitamin C. As a result of this nervous hurried consumption, coupled with a lot of anxiety about the house, I was passing some of those ripe, slow, silent, hot burners, which I had no intention of taking responsibility for. I was easing them out so no one would hear them, while I stood there in the Avis office filling out the rental-car papers. But Forrest was standing next to me at nose level, and he, at the first whiff, just cried out to the whole office, "Dad just farted!" Everyone in the room began to laugh, everyone except me. Kathie was laughing. Marissa was laughing, and all six of the Avis car employees were almost weeping and wetting themselves while they laughed. In fact, Kathie thought one of the women, who was laughing the hardest, and then picked up the phone to talk while she was laughing, was actually calling the Page Six gossip column at the *New York Post* to report what had just happened. Kathie thought she had recognized me from the movie *Beaches* and was reporting this malicious release of gas to the gossip columns. Forrest remembers this story well and laughs as I tell it to him.

Outside the Harbor Deli, we head up the street. We are just three blocks from our home. This last lap takes us by more sweet Victorians and colonial houses with their American flags and white picket fences. We are walking the view we see from our bedroom window. At Sage Street, I stop for a quick look at my favorite odd perspective—that same white steeple with the gold cross that I gaze at while doing my yoga. From this angle, it seems to grow out of that little rise at the top of Sage Street. It looks as though the steeple is literally growing out of the street, and both Forrest and I just stand there staring at it. Then we look at each other and I say, "What does it remind you of, Forrest?" We both say it at once, "The Ku Klux Klan." This was due to the fact that we had both seen the video of *Ghosts of Mississippi* the previous night and still had those Ku Klux Klan associations in our mind. But in fact this truncated white steeple did look like a giant Ku Klux Klan hat resting on the top of Sage Street.

Now, farther up the street, perhaps because of the historic cemetery on our left, Forrest turns to me and says, "Dad, tell me a scary story." He's been so good I want to reward him, but I'm really no good at making up stories, and most of all, scary stories. Anyway, when I was a kid, most so-called scary stories were never really scary to me. So, at first I do what I always do when Forrest asks me to tell him a scary story. I say, "Forrest, just look around you. This is the scary story." I think he sort of knows what I'm talking about, and to some extent I mean it.

I do think there are real and valid fears that fathers can gradually make their sons aware of. We need to teach our children to be afraid of what there is to fear. Fathers need to teach their sons the difference between fear and anxiety. That's a real way into the world. I didn't come into it that way. I came in through Christian Science, where I was taught over and over by my mom and by the Christian Scientist practitioner she hired to pray for me that there was nothing to be afraid of. That there was no "scary story." That made everything both fearful and not fearful.

There does, of course, have to be a balance in everything. I suppose it's important to let your child have the experience of real fear but at the same time not so much real fear that it leaves him traumatized. This is a tricky one. By real fear I don't mean amusement-park rides or Halloween fun houses. That's artificial or theatrical fear. I mean something that occurs in our natural world that is elemental and fearful, like sharks, hurricanes, tornadoes, and AIDS.

As a child, I was always afraid of bears. When my Grandmother Gray and her platonic male friend Harvey would take my brother Rocky to Maine, I would never go, even though they invited me. I wouldn't go because I was deeply afraid of bears. I used to have recurrent dreams of bears chasing me up trees. My grandmother's friend Harvey, an old New England naturalist who once let Rocky and me set a whole field on fire because he knew the wind would blow the flames into the bay, used to tell me that, as far as black bears go, what happens when you run into one is it runs one way and you run the other. I wanted to believe him, but secretly harbored the paranoid fear that somehow the bear would be aware of my deep fear of him and so take advantage of me and just do me in. I couldn't imagine being eaten by a wild beast, and even though Harvey told me they were mostly vegetarians, I couldn't stop imagining them tearing at my young white flesh.

Then one autumn day, when I was a teenager hiking in the White Mountains with my brother Rocky, I had a glorious, spectacular, unexpected meeting with my first bear. My brother and I were coming down from the mountain we had climbed that day and I was well ahead of Rocky when I came around the bend in the trail that ran along a rushing stream. A beautiful big black bear had been drinking from the stream. It was downwind of me and when I rounded the bend in the path the bear just looked up at the same time I looked down and it turned and fled at the same time I turned and ran. Harvey Flint's formula was right. But as I ran with my knees shaking, I kept turning over my shoulder to see the retreat of that wild black beauty. I shall never forget the grace and speed with which that great beast moved. No sad depressed zoo experience could ever touch the natural beauty of that wild free creature retreating through those brilliant autumn leaves. When I got to my brother Rocky on the trail, I told him the story not so much in a state of fear but in a state of awe. In fact, I would venture to say the experience was awesome.

Whether I was aware of it or not, I had always wanted something like that to happen for Forrest at an early age. I wanted something more real and natural, something of this earth to replace or at least rival the more artificial fear of Chucky the doll.

Then it happened quite by chance when Forrest was only three years old. I had him in up to his chest in our little lake outside Brewster. This lake is a wild lake and I love it for that. It contains otters, wide-mouthed bass, Canadian geese, and snapping turtles. I even saw a deer swim full-speed across it once. Then there is the most infamous wild character of all, a big black water snake the local kids have named Sammy. Sammy the Snake does not make appearances all that often, but when he does, it is in the most brazen and dramatic way. He slithers on the surface of the water with his head held high and his forked tongue slashing. He's even been known to charge canoes, just come right out while you're canoeing, just come right at you and try to spit in your face.

So, on this particular summer's day, I was bathing with Forrest in the clear shallow water and I spied Sammy just slithering by, not more than three or four feet from us. It was an excellent view of him. Forrest had his little back to him and didn't see him. I had to make a quick decision. Should I ignore Sammy and let him pass by, or should I point him out to Forrest? I decided in no time and said in a gentle tone, "Forrest. Look. Forrest, look over there. Look over there at Sammy the Snake." Forrest looked, and took it in, felt the fear, and said, "Okay, Dad, we're out of here." That was the first and last time I've ever heard him use the phrase, "We're out of here."

Now he swims in that same lake with great joy and a little fear, caution, and respect.

On our way home, I tell Forrest, "You know, Forrest, my favorite stories are true stories from our lives. Stories about us just living in the world together. But in order to have these stories to tell you, we have to have lived long enough to have a story to tell, and I'm happy to report that you have. You may not remember this story because you were very young, so I'm going to tell you about the time I took you to New Orleans. I had always wanted to go to New Orleans because I love the street music there, and then finally I got a chance to take all of you, the whole family, except for Theo, because he wasn't born yet. It was a Sunday morning. Mom had taken Marissa into a hat shop and I had just bought you a little rubber alligator in a souvenir store. You were about three years old and I had you in your stroller, pushing you around to see that early-morning street scene start to come together. People were just waking up and having their first drinks of the day. We came upon this street jazz band and stopped to listen. There was a clarinet, drums, bass, a trumpet, a trombone, and a banjo. They were just wailing away.

"You got right into it and started beating your rubber alligator, to the rhythm, on your knee. You were keeping perfect time, and what's more, we found out that the alligator had a squeaker in it, so every time you hit your knee to the beat, that alligator let out with a little squeak. So it was 'squeak, squeak, squeak, squeak' as the band played behind you. The band was playing an up-beat version of 'Bye, Bye, Blackbird' and then they went around and all took solos and then it happened, the woman on the clarinet just stopped and turned to you and gestured with her hand, and with the bass and drums going on behind you, you just continued beating that squeaking alligator on your knee. When the band started up again, the whole crowd cheered and clapped for your great rubber-alligator solo. Forrest, you don't know how proud that made your dad to see his son at only three years old do a rubber-alligator solo in the streets of New Orleans."

Once back home, I get Forrest settled in the attic and put *James and the Giant Peach* on the VCR. I stay for a bit until I feel that he is secure and then start down the attic stairs, headed for Kathie's office and our library, to dig at last into my *Encyclopedia Britannica*. At the bottom of the stairs I stop just to stand in that glorious amber light cast by the declining sun in the west. I stand and try to be at home in that sudden silence and peace. I try once again to be still and as I start to drop down into it—into the stillness—Marissa comes to mind. Where is she, I wonder. Perhaps I'm not paying enough attention to her, I think. I speculate on where she might be and what she might be doing. Maybe she is on one of her intense "play dates," as they call them. Funny word, "play date." I don't know when that one slipped into common speech. Maybe sometime around when "I am outta here" and "awesome" crept in. But they are so intense, these "play dates." At eleven years old, they act like obsessive lovers, the way they hang out and play together day and night, and then all that time on the telephone, and then suddenly for no apparent reason, or for some inappropriate remark, it's over. It's just over and done with, just like that. So maybe she's on one of those "play dates" with her latest, or, if not, perhaps she's doing her homework in the guest room or is on the phone to her father talking about what I don't know, but when they talk, it does seem to go on and on for a long time. He does help her with her homework and that's important because I couldn't. I feel so stupid when it comes to lessons. I never really learned anything. The thought of diagramming a sentence, doing fractions, or even spelling a word as simpel as "simpel" puts me in a panic. Just the other day, when I glanced down at Marissa's math book while she was working on it in the kitchen, what I saw made me dizzy and almost sick. The problem read:

The greater of two numbers is seven more than the lesser. Three times the greater number is five more than four times the lesser number. Find the numbers.

This kind of stuff makes my head spin. And I'm afraid Marissa will find me out and judge me as incompetent or dumb. There it is, I am afraid of my stepdaughter's judgment. I feel she's more ruthless and less forgiving of me than she is with her father because I'm her accidental dad. She is not a part of me. So I hold back and wait for her to come to *me* with her needs and her questions. I love to speculate on motivational psychology and eschatology and can usually spar with her on some of those themes. You know, end-of-the-world stuff and why we do and don't do.

Much as I don't like her father because of the way I feel he manipulates her to not approve of us, I do welcome his helping Marissa with her homework. She's doing so well in school with her A average. She's a sharp, smart-thinking girl and I think a lot of that has to do with being an only child of separated (Kathie and Michael were never married) parents. She had to do all this second guessing and personal politicking to make her way in and out of two parents that basically hate each other and only communicate through lawyers. It's sad, and I truly believe Kathie when she tells me that, for the sake of Marissa, she wants to relate to Marissa's father. Kathie claims she doesn't understand why Michael, Marissa's dad, doesn't like her, but I think she really knows. It seems Kathie was supporting Michael, who was a struggling graffiti artist but wasn't going to his studio all the time she thought he was. No, he was not going to his studio, but he was going elsewhere, and then he ran off with one of the "elsewheres." Kathie told me that it was all a real surprise to her, and of course to Marissa. Kathie was working three jobs to support the family, and one day she came home to Michael, who was sitting out on the porch surrounded by garbage bags filled with his clothes, and he just told her he was leaving her for another woman. Just like that.

Marissa was only two. Kathie told me that when Michael left, she and Marissa just broke down and cried together. Then, after a few days, Kathie realized that she was grateful to be rid of him. She realized she didn't have the courage to break up, so was glad he did it. Then when he wanted to come back, Kathie said, "No." So I guess that might produce some rage in him. It would pretty much do it for me. They had also planned to move to New York City together and Kathie ended up doing that on her own with Marissa. In New York she started her own business and started raising Marissa on her own.

Kathie had never heard of me and my monologue work before Marissa's father introduced her to it. One night, instead of going to a party, he wanted to stay home and watch a video tape of my monologue *Swimming to Cambodia*. He was "a big fan," but is now no longer a fan.

After seeing the video of *Swimming to Cambodia*, Kathie became a fan and booked me at a performance space she was working at in Rochester, New York. That's where I met and went to bed with her for the first time.

So I can sort of understand what Marissa's father might be angry about, but it's not as though he doesn't have a life of his own. He's back in school, he has a wife who pretty much supports him, and he's a father to a new son. Yet, when he calls on the phone, I can hear so much rage and anger in his voice. You can hear all that rage caught in his throat, and when I answer, I always feel like asking, "Michael, what are you so angry about?" But I don't. I don't say anything of the sort. I just play mister nice polite guy. Then when Marissa goes to visit her father it's like an iron curtain comes down. No word gets in and no word gets out. She won't take or return our phone calls. We've given up calling because we've come to understand that Michael and his wife make it too difficult for Marissa to feel free on the telephone. So Kathie, not being able to stand the rejection, writes letters instead.

Marissa's doing well. She's really doing well in spite of this major life hassle. I first met Marissa when she was only three. She was very cute and very sophisticated then. Kathie brought her to a party I was at in a loft in downtown Manhattan. I think by this time, although she had never met me, she was aware of my existence. She knew someone named Spalding Gray had been calling her mom a lot on the phone as well as paying occasional visits. Only Marissa, for whatever reason, could not quite handle my name, so instead of Spalding Gray she called me Splendid Café, which I thought was a perfect stage name for me if I ever needed one.

I remember Kathie brought her into the party in her arms. Marissa looked so cute, bright-eyed, and vulnerable. She was carrying a clipboard and claiming to be Madonna's publicist. Marissa and I had instant, intense eye contact as soon as Kathie carried her through the door. At that moment, I sort of knew that she sort of knew who I was. I was "the rival." I was clearly the rival for her mother's love. Then I just looked her straight in

the eye and said, "You and I are going to have a nice little talk together. I'm going to go into the kitchen to sit
down, and when you're ready, you come in and we'll
talk." She never came in.

When Marissa was six, we all moved into my little
loft together. That was a close, chaotic time. There was
never a dull moment, which suited some fabulistic
drama-queen side of me. The more dramatically chaotic,
the better, and what I quickly discovered was that
Marissa, like me, was also a real drama queen. Marissa
was like a strange mirror to me. We both dramatized our
lives. It was as though we both proudly thought that life,
indeed, was a rehearsal. We both thought that life was a
rehearsal for the perfect story and the perfect audience.

I remember shortly after we moved into our Sag Harbor house, I was home taking care of Forrest and Marissa
and I heard this crashing sound on the attic stairs. I ran
upstairs to find Marissa sprawled out at the bottom of the
attic stairs. As soon as I saw her, I knew that the fall had
all been an act. I knew that she had pretended to fall
down the stairs, but instead of calling her on it I responded by going into my own version of my act. I went
right into my counter-act. I went down to the kitchen
and got an ice pack and brought it up and put it on
Marissa's head, pretending to be nursing her back to con-

sciousness. Marissa and I both often act as though we are living. Acting as though you're living is often much safer than really living.

Then I noticed a big change in Marissa the day her father called to announce to her that he and his wife had just given birth to a son. At that moment, on the phone, Marissa understood that she was no longer the center of that family configuration. She had to deal now with yet another half brother. From the dining room, I listened to her conversation on the phone with her father. I could tell she was upset but she acted polite and told him that she loved him, just before she hung up. Then she ran upstairs to the attic, and I heard her up there burst into tears. I heard her wailing. I went upstairs and stood at the bottom of the attic stairs and just listened. I listened to her cry and didn't go up. I knew what I heard was not an act and belonged to her.

Shortly after this incident, Marissa's great-grand-mother died. The funeral of Kathie's grandmother, for me, was quite an event. Not only was it the first death in our new family, it was the first open-casket funeral I've ever been a part of, and it seemed to go on for days. It started with the viewing of the body in a coffin, which was an unexpected shock for me. When I first laid eyes on the recomposed corpse of Kathie's grandmother, I ex-

pected it to just sit up and say, "Please pass the choco-
lates," or something like that. I could not quite take it in
and process all this lifelessness in a body that was so re-
constructed to look like it was simply napping. Marissa,
of all the people there, dealt with it so well, and she had
only recently turned ten. She stood by the open coffin
and interviewed all the various relatives who came to
view what was left of her great-grandmother. After doing
that, the following day, when people gathered for their
last look before the casket was taken to the church,
Marissa read a poem that she had composed. I think
the poem was based on the interviews she'd done the
previous day as well as her reaction to touching her
great-grandmother's corpse. The poem went:

> *I just touched my Nona*
> *She was cold still and no life*
> *No more smiles on nice warm happy days*
> *No more joy that filled the air with love*
> *No more meatballs in Florida*
> *Oh Nona, you are gone gone gone and we know*
> *not where.*

As soon as Marissa finished reading her poem, everyone rushed to her, an ex-nun, an ex-priest, and Kathie's

mother. And Kathie's mother said, "But, Marissa, we all know where Nona has gone. She's in heaven now, dear." Marissa just turned to all of them and said, "Heaven? What a bore."

What a strange, strict, quick imagination Marissa has. I remember when we were renting that house in Martha's Vineyard for the summer and we kept hearing this thumping sound on the roof. It was as if there was a dog up there running around. Then Kathie and I discovered it was a very large neurotic seagull just running back and forth on the roof. Shortly thereafter, we were having a dinner party and Marissa had just finished telling her version of Carlos's joke about the skeleton walking into a bar and ordering a glass of beer and a mop. Marissa's version went, "A skeleton walks into a bar and orders a glass of wine and a broom." She had just finished saying that when we heard the sound of the seagull on the roof. We heard it thrashing around on the roof, and one of the women at the party said, "Whatever is that?" and Marissa answered, "It's a seagull and I don't like it one bit." To which our guest replied, "And why not, Marissa?" Marissa answered, "Because it's not paying rent."

Later in the party, the same woman was talking intensely about her deep belief in the possibility for human change. "We can all change if we really want to," she said, to which Marissa replied, "Yes, I believe in change. Look at the Unabomber, for example. He was a professor and he became a bomber."

Well, all this leads me to believe Marissa might make a very good trial lawyer one day. She seems set on getting into Yale. Her grades are really good and she is an absolute purist about keeping her mind sharp and clear. No drugs for this young lady. No. No. Just the other day Kathie was pumping gas into our Volvo at a self-service pump and some gasoline spilled on her shoe, so when she got into the car, it made the inside reek of gasoline. Marissa, sure that the smell would cause her brain cells to die, rode with her head out the window for an hour. She will survive and thrive. There is no doubt in my mind about that.

Going into Kathie's office—our library—I am happy to find Kathie not there. She is, I think, most likely out for a walk with Theo. That gives me the wonderful chance now to collapse into the couch and be alone at last with the *Encyclopedia Britannica*. Those encyclopedias line the top shelf of our red built-in bookcase. They are a regal and noble collection, purchased one day on a whim from a somewhat sad, down-in-the-dumps door-to-door salesman in search of people who still related to books. Yes, these books are great objects. They are bound in heavy burgundy-and-black leather, with gold lettering. I am amazed to find they are pretty much lined up in alphabetical order. Now, thinking in that order, I go for "D" first, to look up "deer." I scan the passage and find nothing on "poop" or "size of excrement." Next I go for "E" and am somewhat amazed to find forty-seven pages on Earth, but nothing about why we can't feel the motion of its spinning. I start to feel sleepy and stupid. Maybe I'm just an unconscious Luddite. I'm so computer illiterate. Here I am a writer and I never learned to type. If I had a computer now, all I'd have to do is plug in "poop" and "spin" and I'd be home free. But I do love my books, I think, as I look around the room at my collection. I think of how many times I've read, over and over, these same books and underlined all my favorite passages in red. I do love these books as objects. I love to take them down and handle them, read a section, and then put them back in their place. And as I look around the room at the titles this particular day, I am struck by how many of these books have the word "death" in the title: *The Denial of Death*, *Life Against Death*, *The Tibetan Book of Living and Dying, Death Be Not Proud, Death in Venice, How We Die*, and many more. With the exception of *The Tibetan Book of Living and Dying*, most of these books are more about dealing with the mystery of death, rather than attempts to explain it. They are about our reaction to not knowing. As I sit there, I realize, as I have before, that most of our behavior, our morals, our ethics, our everyday behavior, is based on how we react to our limited awareness of death. Ever since I first read Dostoevsky, I have thought about how absurdly courageous it is to try to lead a moral life in the face of no external order. If God is dead, or at least silent, then all things, with the exception of immortality, are open to human possibility. For me, the existential moralists have always been my heroes. They seem to have the courage to try to do the right thing in the face of what appears to be endless relativity. They say, if nothing matters and all things are relative, then they will make it matter, and they will make it matter in a positive, human way. For me, the existentialists are freethinkers and not operating out of a more systematized ideology. On the other hand, *The Tibetan Book of Living and Dying*, a more popular book in these times, is for me a more hellfire-and-brimstone book and harder to take. At its worst, it's a hierarchical and systematized ideological diatribe of all the horrors of after-death states and how you can be saved from these hell realms only by the proper lama or priest. This book reminds me very much of James Joyce's take on Catholicism in his descriptions of hell in *Portrait of the Artist as a Young Man*. *The Tibetan Book of Living and Dying* is a book I just cannot read. I've tried, but I can't do it. It makes me feel like I have to have a Ph.D. to die. It makes me feel like I have to go back to school to learn the right way to die, and this is very discouraging, because I've never really learned anything in my life. I'm just no good at lessons. I was born into the world without a priest or lama guiding me in. Why, pray tell, can't I go gracefully out the same way I came in? That's what I want to know as I sit there starting to nod, as I feel that late-afternoon stupefaction creep over me. And then there are all those books that are so popular now about near-death experiences. I can't fathom the popularity of them, or understand how they make it onto the best-seller lists. I remember talking to my friend Ken about this phenomenon and asking him for his take on these books and he said, "Well, Spald, remember this: there's 'near-death' and then there's **death**!" And he actually scared me. Ken screamed the word *death* so loud that I almost fell out of the canoe we were both in.

But, I think as I look around the room at my books

again, I think I would be embarrassed to have my sons know how much more I have thought about not being here than I have about being here. I think about how much I have allowed myself to get caught up in regret and how I've paid more attention to my fantasy of what didn't happen than I have to the memory of what did. I think of all my elsewhereness.

I do think these old patterns of regret and fantasies of the non-event were old ways of staying in touch with my mom, who is definitely not happening anymore. Much of that has changed for me now that I've become a stepfather and a dad. I'm more present now, but the disembodied voice of death still visits me every day to remind me that I will die, and the idea of that, of not being here forever, just wipes me out.

One thing I feel sure of is that we are . . . or I, this me, this all-of-me that sits here now, this total receiver, will never know not being here. Aspects may linger and be confused as a chicken with its head cut off, but the whole bird will never know what it is to not be. If there are separate realities, this me that sits here now will never walk through them. Perhaps that's where all that elsewhereness comes in. Being elsewhere in your mind is a big working metaphor for not being here.

So, what do I tell my boys when they come to me with their questions on death? Forrest already has. He started asking me about death before he was four and I told him that everyone who is born must one day die. Then I told him that the funny thing about that . . . or odd thing, because death is rarely funny, is that everyone knows they're going to die but no one really believes it.

This is a big and important fact, I told him. This is, in fact, what I consider the *reality* of this world. He seemed to take this in. I don't know what Forrest did with it, but he listened and he took it in. When my friend Ken heard that I had told Forrest this about death, he said that it might have been a big mistake because Forrest would just end up thinking, why bother? Forrest would end up deeply depressed at six years old.

My brother Channing told me that when his daughter Amanda first came into her eschatological dilemma, he just told her about reincarnation, he told her that she would be reborn, and that put her at ease. I took a more brutal route with Forrest and he seems to be all right. But I did notice that at no age did he believe in Santa Claus, and I wondered if that had to do with his early doubts about supreme beings.

I remember when Forrest was first talking and he first

saw Santa Claus, he said, "Santa Clock scare me." After that, he just went from fear and distrust to an almost so-phisticated indifference.

So it's not so much what should I tell him but what can I tell him that would come from my heart? Could I tell him that we are pretty much in charge of our own destinies? That the only meaning is the meaning we make, or that the meaning we make is equal to the meaning we take?

Here is what I am trying to pinpoint as I sit here in my late-afternoon fuzziness. Here is what I am trying to pin down for myself. The question for me is, when did I first really realize that I was going to die forever? I think it was that night when I woke up to find Mom and Dad try-ing to calm my brother Rocky down. I think Rocky was about nine years old, which would have made me about six. I woke up to find my brother standing on his bed, holding his throat with both hands, blue in the face and crying for help. He kept crying, "Help, help, I can't breathe." Mom and Dad were both trying to calm him down. To me, it looked like he was strangling himself and that was why he couldn't breathe, but any way you looked at it, it was scary. Then at last Mom and Dad calmed Rocky down and Dad went back to bed and Mom turned out the light and sat there in the dark beside Rocky. I just lay there listening and staring up at the only light in the room, the fluorescent decals of the moon and the stars on the ceiling. I lay there and Rocky started in and said, "Mom, when I die, will it be forever?" And Mom answered him with this beautiful calm tone of voice so simple and slow. She just said, "Yes, dear." Then Rocky said it again and again, and each time he asked her, he would add another "forever," and each time Mom would give this steady, slow, affirmative response. Looking back on that now, I think how odd it was that my mother, who was a woman who constantly proclaimed her belief in an afterlife with Jesus Christ, never once tried to sell Rocky her vision of heaven on that particular night. Perhaps I went to sleep before she did it, I don't know. What I almost know, what I have inklings of, is that my brother Rocky stole my fear of death from me. He was so afraid, there was no room for my fear. I mean, I couldn't imagine also hitting my parents with it at the same time Rocky was doing such an incredible demonstration of it. There was hardly any room left for my fears.

Most of all, I remember lying there in the dark, going down that long passage of forever and ever and ever with him. I think I needed to hear Mom say, "Everything is going to be all right, dear," but she didn't. Or at least I didn't hear it. The other thing that got me was watching my brother not being able to catch his breath, not being able to breathe. That's the "scary story" for me. That's the scary story I couldn't tell Forrest when he asked me for a scary story. It's about how we all are going—more or less have to—one day suffocate, asphyxiate, stop breathing. That the most natural, automatic, totally taken-for-granted flowing-in-and-out event that we know, our breathing, will one day stop. Help! We won't be able to breathe. That is indeed the "scary story" for me and a version of it was illustrated most vividly in a Dutch film called *The Vanishing*. That was a real horror film for me. I will never forget it.

It goes like this. This guy is traveling with his girlfriend and she gets kidnapped. He is totally devastated by this and devotes his life to investigating her disappearance. It goes something like that, but it doesn't really matter, it's the last image in the film that got me. So it goes that he finds the kidnapper and they have drinks together and he says that he will take him to the same place his missing girlfriend is. Of course, what the guy doesn't know is that his drink is drugged, and he passes out. Now here is where the genius of the film comes in: the next shot is of him coming to, and because it's a new shot, and a close-up, you as a viewer are as disoriented as he is. Where are we? you wonder. Then the camera pulls back enough to reveal that he is in a coffin. He has been buried alive! This feels so horrible because as a viewer, or at least I as a viewer, made the discovery at the same time he did, so I could almost feel his hands as my hands as they pushed, pounded, and hammered on that forever-sealed coffin. What a horror that was for me. I felt I couldn't breathe. Then the camera pulls away to give some diabolical comic relief. We see the kidnapper and his family having a delightful cookout and family picnic right on top of the two graves. So it's the guy pounding in the coffin below and the happy children eating bratwurst above. Oh, that scene in the coffin will stay with me forever. It brings back that feeling of suffocation, of breath stopping. That scary story I can't even begin to tell Forrest.

Then just the other day I had a hopeful fantasy. What if, when we are dying, instead of our breath stopping, it instead shifts from us into the breath of the Universe. Yes, I suddenly had a peaceful sense that the whole universe was actually breathing and that at our last breath we can, if we choose, breathe into it and become one with the great swelling and retracting breath of the universe. I felt almost hopeful. I thought that maybe that's a positive image I can give Forrest to work with, my fantasy of what is beyond the apparent death of breath.

Then in no time I thought, who really wants to become a part of an eternal egoless universal energy field? It feels too much like spiritual communism. I couldn't lay that on my son. No, I think, now tired of thinking about it, all I can do is hold him and say, "We don't know, it's a mystery. I love you and everything is going to be all right."

It's odd but that voice that says, "Everything is going to be all right," that's the one I choke on. I have no problem telling Forrest that I love him, and then when I try to say "Everything is going to be all right," I feel so distant from myself, so faraway and down the hall. Do I remember that phrase coming from my mother and father? No, not really. Mom told us that God and Jesus loved us. As far as my father went, Mom always seemed to be his emotional go-between. She'd be the one who told me that my father loved me and was proud of me. I never remember it coming from him.

Now the late-afternoon stupor is taking me over and I begin to fall into my nodding nap. Into my nodding nap the disembodied voice of death enters. This voice is as fearful to me as Chucky the doll is to Forrest, only I can save Forrest from the fear of Chucky, and no one can save me from the fear that this disembodied voice of death engenders in me.

The disembodied voice of death whispers, "Hello, Spalding, here I am again, just as you are relaxing, to remind you that all that you think you know and feel and remember will one day disappear forever. Gone gone forever gone. And all the substance that surrounds you now will cave in like so much sand and sea to fill the place where you once were. It will all be as though you never existed."

I anxiously protest with, "But my kids, my children will remember me. That's something, isn't it?"

And the voice says, "Come on, guy, you already know my response to that one."

"Don't call me 'guy,' " I say. "My name is Spalding."

"Oh, really? You mean you're not just 'the-thing-in-itself'? Oh no, of course not, you're one of those guys with one of those fancy first last names. That gives you the illusion that you're somehow special, and just because you never met another Spalding, you somehow won't go the way of all the other names that start in the air and end on stone. Okay, Spalding, if you need to hear it again, I will do my old routine. Here goes, 'All things are subject to change. Your children will pass and disappear just as you will. Even your sun will pass as your son did and will one day burn out. No one will be watching anymore. No one will be left to say, "Here all of us have been." And it will all be as though none of this ever happened.' In fact, doesn't it already feel a little bit like that now?"

"Oh, disembodied voice of death," I say, "you've got me by the throat and I can't breathe. What can I do in the face of this concrete wall you've built for me? What can I do besides remember, and obsessively recollect over and over again?"

And the voice answers sweetly, "Try enjoying life for a change. See if you can, and remember, tend your gardens. By all means, tend your gardens."

"But I'm not really the gardener. Kathie does all that stuff."

And the voice responds, "Remember how you used to say, 'If I am going to have children, let it be late in life, so I'll be dead by the time they are teenagers'? Well, that gives you very little time. Take your boys fishing. Love your children and teach them to fish or organize. Help organize to shut down that nuclear reactor. You can do it, guy, Mister Spalding, and forget about me. I can never be known. I can only be encountered. Then one day when you least expect it, surprise! You will meet the inevitable, blend with it, and accept it. Here there is no choice. It's inevitable and it's elemental, Mister Spalding. Now don't say another word. You're oh-so-cozy with words. I shouldn't even be talking to you. Remember this, there is the disembodied voice of death and then there is *death*!"

I hear that gigantic word *death* echo through my nap and then for a moment all is dark and silent. There is almost no awareness. I am like a patient etherized upon a table. No report to you from me. No me.

I burst awake like Ebenezer Scrooge on Christmas morning. I can smell the dinner Kathie is preparing in the kitchen. It smells like a delicious lamb stew, and I feel the word "delicious" in my head and it feels like a scrumptious ripe fruit. I hear the warm buzz of the family below and I realize it's cocktail hour! Oh, for a drink or two or three to ease me into night and forgetfulness. Oh, what the warm glow of the family circle and a little vodka and tomato juice won't do to dispel the disembodied voice of death.

Downstairs, I walk into the kitchen hubbub. Theo is in his high chair, doing his big enthusiastic baby jerk, looking like a battery-operated child. Marissa is trying to bake some Jiffy puff rolls, and Kathie is perfecting the lamb stew. It all smells like "Home for the holidays." Forrest is down from *James and the Giant Peach*, and he is sitting at the kitchen counter, drawing a variety of made-up monsters. I get out the makings for my Bloody Marys and begin to mix.

Once I get my first drink made, I go into the living room to get a fire started in the fireplace. The wood is good and dry and is off and burning in a perfect, picturesque frame. I sit in the wingback chair with my drink in hand and stare into the fire. The first three sips take me down into cozy, mellow forgetfulness. All of a sudden, I don't remember everything, and sitting there, I fantasize that I'm a famous bachelor writer just in-between love affairs and working on my new novel at a New Hampshire writers' retreat. I fantasize that I am in my study drinking and reflecting on the manifestations of my genius.

Then, when this fantasy bubble breaks, I go out into the kitchen and play at being the "family man." I mix and intermingle with the children. I stir Kathie's lamb stew with a long wooden spoon. I squeeze Theo's cheek. Then I go back into the living room to sit down again by the fire.

The phone rings and it's Marissa's father. Annoyed, I call out to Kathie, "Why does he always call at dinnertime?"

Marissa takes the portable phone upstairs, as if she can talk to her father only in secret. "What's she doing that for?" I say to Kathie. "Why, has she got so many secrets with him? What are they talking about?" Kathie ignores me. I want to pick up the extension phone and listen in, but I don't. Forrest asks me for a Virgin Mary and I gladly make it for him. "Dad, could I tell you something? Why do they call a virgin a virgin?" And I say, "Forrest, in this case it means 'tomato juice without vodka.'"

I make myself another Bloody Mary and then take Theo out of his high chair and toss him into the air. His eyes shine down on me and bathe me like a warm sun.

Kathie asks me to help her begin moving things into the dining room. She asks me to move Theo's high chair in and to call Marissa down to set the table. I go to the bottom of the stairs and call up, "Marissa, please get off the phone and come down here to set the table."

At the top of the stairs, Marissa calls down, "How much are you going to pay me?"

Her response triggers something in me and I go off, shouting, "That's enough, young lady! You're not working in a hotel! You're part of a family. Get down here and help out!"

I am amazed at how much the children have liberated my anger so late in my life. I could never express pure rage before. I was always passive-aggressive in my previous long relationships with the two other women in my life. They owned the anger in our relationship, or I let them own it. I gave it over to them. If I was angry about something, I would provoke the anger in them, and then all I would get coming back at me was my misplaced anger at them. In other words, my passive-aggressive anger got converted into their active anger.

Now the children have liberated a purer, more direct anger in me, and I find I can also turn it on Kathie, when it's appropriate (I usually can feel the appropriateness of the situation) without guilt. This has been a big breakthrough for me at a very late age. I think it's healthy.

Marissa is down now and is doing her version of setting the table. She's slapping the forks and napkins down with attitude, like a slave princess. I call Forrest in and Kathie carries Theo in and puts him in his high chair. Then she says, "Oops, I smell a poopie diaper." Forrest quickly retorts, "Don't say that word 'poopie' when I'm about to eat." To which I quickly reply, "Okay, Forrest, now this is a good example of 'the word in context.' The word 'poopie' becomes repulsive to you because it comes in context with your sitting here about to eat. You see, in the context of the dinner-table setting, this word 'poopie' becomes an inappropriate and unpleasant word for you. Now for me, on the other hand, I don't mind it. For me, to my nose, the smell of Theo's poopie diaper reminds me of an exotic overripe French cheese."

In outrageous disgust, Marissa interjects, "Spalding! Please . . ."

To which I say, "Well now, Marissa, you are not trying to censor me at my table, are you?"

Marissa comes right back at me with, "What do you mean, your table? I thought we were a family here. Isn't it really *our* table? And don't I have a right to my opinion?"

Then Kathie interjects with, "Please, Spalding, you are treating Marissa like an all-knowing adult. She's still really only a child."

"Oh, really?" I say, feeling some of that good old pure rage coming up. "Well, she is certainly acting like an all-knowing something."

"Well, maybe I am," Marissa retorts and sets off a ping-pong ball effect between us both.

"Maybe you're not," I say.

"Maybe I am," she says.

And so it goes back and forth, back and forth like two kids fighting, until Kathie interrupts to point to Theo. Somehow, perhaps through the devilish hand of Forrest, Theo has gotten hold of my little half-lens reading glasses and he has put them on, which makes him look like a little Truman Capote. We all turn to him and laugh. This innocent spectacle has instantly altered the whole mood of the dining room. We have all been re-duced, or rather elevated, to laughter. It feels so good, until I suddenly come down and see and correct Forrest's sitting posture at the table. "Forrest," I say, "please do not sit sideways in your chair. Please sit around squarely at the table, as though you're going to stay awhile and eat. Also use your fork, please, and not your hands."

Forrest completely surprises me and takes me off-guard with, "You're not my boss. You can't boss me around."

This retort activates another one of those rage triggers in me and I say, "Oh yeah? If I'm not the boss, who is?"

At the same time I say this, I can hear myself saying it and trying to check myself. I have a self-conscious image of myself and wonder if this is how the children will re-member me. I wonder if I had too much to drink before dinner. I think how I never wanted to have children in the first place because I never wanted to have to act like a cop. I never wanted to be someone else's superego. I just wanted to be a sweet, old mellow uncle figure for someone else's kids. Now I'm in the thick of it and there is no way out. I think of myself renouncing everything except running a ski lift in Colorado. I see myself blankly staring out the window at an endless snowscape. The children have at last outnumbered the parents. It's three to two, and I go back to my childhood table in my memory. My mom always insisted that we start dinner in a silent prayer. So we'd all be coming out of a nice silence which always shifted the mood into a more harmonious and peaceful state. My father pretty much forbid any general discussion about anything. I think he felt any discussion was a form of argument. He told us how to hold our forks, he asked us what we had for lunch at school, and he occasionally gave us advice like, "Remember, all things are relative, and whatever you do, marry a wealthy woman."

I don't remember any jokes or much laughter at our dinner table. Once, when my younger brother, who was about eleven at the time, piped up and said, "Dad, Teddy Waterman told me a joke today that I didn't understand. He asked me if his hair was combed and when I said yes, he said, 'How can you see through my pants?' What does that mean, Dad?" No one said a word. We all just went on eating our meat and potatoes. Then, after a long silence, Dad said, "I'll explain that to you later, my friend." I don't think he ever got around to explaining it.

So this—what I can only call dinner-table repression—went on for years, up until Rocky and I were teenagers. It was around that time that Mom started to give way under years of inadequate self-expression and she began to develop a phenomenal intestinal gas buildup. She began to let loose at the table. She would just let go with these incredible, uninhibited rippers that sounded like someone was tearing up canvas sheets under the table. I mean, they were solid surprise rippers. Then she would begin to laugh at my father's huffy, shocked, and disgusted reaction. She would laugh so hard she'd wet her pants. By the time she got as far as wetting her pants, Dad would be out of there. He'd be off in the living room, where he would just sit there steaming in his armchair while pretending to read the paper. The *Providence Journal* would be held high in front of his face, like a paper wall to his family.

"Forrest, I don't want to be your boss. I want to be your guide. Now please sit around at the table and use your fork to eat. Now let's all eat Kathie's wonderful lamb stew. Oh yes, it smells so good, doesn't it, kids? I swear, your mom could be a cook in a gourmet restaurant if she wanted to." Marissa and Forrest begin to eat.

Marissa takes one bite and stops to pull a small fleck of something out of her mouth. "What's this weird spice?" she asks.

I groan and say, "Marissa, that is not a spice. That's an herb. It's rosemary and it's from your mother's herb garden."

To which Marissa retorts, "From the garden? Has it been sterilized?"

This sets me off. "Marissa," I say, "you are from the garden. You are from the earth. Have you been sterilized?"

"Calm down," Kathie says. "It's not worth fighting over food."

"I've decided I want Lunchables instead," Marissa says as Forrest chimes in, "Me, too, Mom. Me too. Lunchables for me too!"

"Oh my God, Kathie, you're not going to let them eat Lunchables when we have this great lamb stew?"

Marissa hesitates for a second, somewhat stunned by my rage. Then Kathie says, "We can always freeze the stew." Kathie gives the two kids the nod for Lunchables. I am really beside myself now as I watch Marissa and Forrest bring in what I think of as a refrigerated, overpriced food kit. There they are, opening their little Lunchable packets right at the table. Making up what looks like a little mini-pizza, and it's all cold! The sauce is cold, the pizza dough is cold, and it all leaves me cold. I pour another glass of wine and try to enjoy my lamb stew. Kathie says, "Oh, come on, Spalding, don't fret. If they don't like it, they don't have to eat it. I'm not into force-feeding. Let's just let it go." In the middle of all this, Forrest pipes in with one last dig, "You're food-obsessed, Dad." Kathie catches me just in time before I go off on him. She takes my hand and, holding it, says, "Let's talk about something else. Let's talk about something that happened in school today. Marissa, what happened to you today?"

Marissa's whole attitude changes and she just sparks up and says, "Well, Holly Marin walked home with a boy today." To which Kathie says, "Oh great. What's wrong with that? Don't you just have a little bit of a crush on some boy?"

Marissa sits up ramrod-straight and very forwardly says, "No, not at all. I'm free of all that."

Then Forrest says, "No, Mom, she has a crush on Leonardo."

"Not anymore," Marissa retorts. "I found out that he's bisexual and he smokes."

"Well," I say, "then what would be your ideal crush situation, Marissa?"

Marissa just shifts moods and goes into this very dramatic story line. She says, "Well, I see it this way. I get a scholarship to Oxford and while I'm there I just happen to go to a Spice Girls concert where I just happen to get noticed by Prince Harry. Prince Harry falls instantly in love with me, and his brother, Prince William, gets so jealous that he steals me away. Then I end up marrying Prince William and I become Queen, Marissa the First!" Then she takes a rest and says, after about two bites of her pizza Lunchables, "May I be excused?" Kathie excuses her and she gets up and carries her plate out into the kitchen, and Forrest follows.

"Wow," I say to Kathie. "Where did she learn that 'May I be excused' stuff? Did she learn that from her father? I've never seen that before."

Now the dinner table is two people calmer. The overhead light is low and the table is lit by two candles. It's all very soft and romantic. Theo seems happy with his baby food and some handfuls of white rice. Kathie and I begin to unwind. We both have some more Chardonnay and I at last begin to feel the wine relaxing me, and easing me down.

Marissa and Forrest have gone out into the living room to play in front of the fire. If either of them is in the mood, they might put a CD on our little Bose in the corner. If Marissa wins out, as she usually does, it will be Spice Girls, but if Forrest wins, or, should I say, if Marissa gives over, we will hear Hanson.

We hear neither. As Kathie and I sit there in the dining room sipping our wine, we hear a strange new theme emanating from the living room and Kathie cries out, "Oh, wow! It's Chumbawamba."

Kathie and I can't resist. She grabs baby Theo out of the high chair and we go into the living room to join Forrest and Marissa in their dance to Chumbawamba. The whole room is filled with a great variety of moves. Marissa is doing balletic leaps across the living room. Forrest is spinning. I take Theo from Kathie's arms and leave her walking like an Egyptian while I spin Theo around and dance with him. The fire in the fireplace is still burning well and the whole family is dancing. The whole family is dancing to Chumbawamba.

After our dance, we all go downtown for ice cream. Kathie gets out that great gray 1948 perambulator she bought at a yard sale and puts Theo in it and we begin our family trip. The streets are empty. When we walk out, it feels to me like we are walking through a Hollywood soundstage for the movie of *Our Town*. It feels like our town, and we are the only people in it. I feel we're the only family in town, and I do believe we are the only family that walks anywhere at night.

By the time we get back, Theo is asleep, so Kathie goes upstairs with him to lay him down in his crib. Forrest and Marissa go up to the attic to get ready for bed, and I stay downstairs to clean up the rest of the dishes.

When I come up to the attic to see how things are going, Kathie has just finished reading two books to Forrest and is saying good night to him and getting ready to move on to Marissa, who is reading to herself at the far end of the attic.

I turn out Forrest's bed light and lie down beside him. We are both looking up through the skylight at the stars. It's a clear, moonless October night and the stars are brilliant even through the skylight. There are no cities or shopping centers close by to light up and obliterate the night sky. I am suddenly very thankful to be living where we live. We lie there for a while in luscious reflective silence. Then Forrest breaks the silence with "Dad, you see the stars?"

"Yes, Forrest. Aren't they incredible?"

"But, Dad, what's on the other side of them?"

"That's a mystery, Forrest. We don't know that."

A little more agitated, Forrest says, "No, no, Dad. You see the stars? What's beyond them?"

And I repeat, "That's a mystery, Forrest. That's one of the mysteries here on Earth that I don't think we will ever solve."

"No, no, Dad," he says, more animated now, his hands shaping the air above him. "You see the stars, Dad? Well, what's on the other side? What's beyond them?"

I look over at him and say once again, "Forrest, we don't know that. That's a mystery. Now you look at me and tell me what I've been telling you about the stars."

Forrest just looks over at me and with this unexpected, and unusual, direct eye contact he just says, "Pee pee, shit burgers, ka-ka, pee bone, penis breath!"

I kiss him good night and get up to walk out of the attic but he stops me with one last gem. "Dad, before you go, could I tell you something? I am so glad you met Mom or I would have been stuck inside a sperm forever."

I laugh and tell him good night and then go to the far end of the attic to kiss Marissa. She is lying in bed reading, alternating between *Teen People* and *Wives of Henry the Eighth*. I kiss her on the cheek and go to Kathie, who has been waiting for me at the top of the attic stairs.

We fall into bed together. I kiss her, turn out my table lamp, and fall back into darkness, while she keeps her lamp on to read. I think, no video or books for me, I'm wasted. Here it is only ten-fifteen in the evening and I'm wasted, and I didn't even go to work. I don't know how people do it. I don't know how people raise families and work at the same time. What's more, why would they want to do it? With only one life to live, why bring more life into the world to be responsible for? It's absurd. It's ridiculous, I think. Why complicate your life with more life that you are ultimately responsible for? I love my children, but they could only be accidents born out of a kind of blind passion. I could never have had a child if I had to think about it. I know that now. I also think of all the single, working mothers and I think, oh, pray, pray for the single mothers. How do they do it? Bless them. I lie there wondering where or what I'd be if I was not here in this bed, and for the first time in my life perhaps, not a lot of fantasy comes to mind. It's not been a bad day, really. The thought of it happening over and over again is just too much for me to let in. It makes me think of Camus' myth of Sisyphus and how I have to find that book in my library, one of the books without death in the title, and read it again.

I once again think it's not been a bad day. After all, think of all that could have gone wrong. And I do. I begin to think of all the things that could go wrong. I imagine the Millstone Reactor melting down. I see rogue asteroids hovering in dark space all around us. I think of all the new drug-resistant bacteria. I see a vision of the Islamic Jihad burning American flags. I see my scrotal arteries being crushed by my bicycle seat. I hear Theo falling down the attic stairs. I think of all the pesticides in our drinking water and of all the Long Island cancer clusters, including a rise in childhood leukemia. I wonder about the Y2K factor and if I should take all my money out of the bank, convert it into twenty-dollar bills, and bury it in our back yard. I worry about Kathie coming down with chronic fatigue syndrome. Oh my God, save me from that. I almost find myself trying to actually pray. How would I ever get the children off to school each day over and over again until death do us part?

These images of chance disasters and ill luck begin to spin and blend together like so many weekly catastrophe covers on *Time* or *Newsweek*. They begin to mix and blend into a blurry, colorful wheel, like a wheel of fortune or like a Tibetan wheel of living and dying. And as that wheel begins to spin, it spins and spins into a blur of black that turns into an ink-black river flowing in my mind, flowing toward the edge of all existence. The river flows and drops off the edge forever. There is no bottom to the abyss that this river falls into, and in this river I see the sad, lost, horror-stricken faces of all the recent dead. I see all the ones that have left us forever. I see friends and loved ones. I see celebrities and strangers. It looks like a sad, freaky Hieronymus Bosch vision combined with the movie *The Fly*, because the heads of the people remind me of that scientist's head stuck on the body of a fly. Also, the heads and faces are crying out to me in that small, high human voice, the voice of the scientist in that movie. They're crying, "Help! Help me! Save me! This should not be! Save me from the end of me!"

Now, to my shock and horror, our whole house is in motion. It has ripped away from its brick-and-stone foundation and is now floating down the ink-black river with all the crying faces, all the crying heads. The house, our house, seems to be alive and breathing as I feel each child sleeping and breathing in their rooms, sleeping and breathing like small independent lungs, lungs of love. At the same time, they are lungs of the house and the house is a body floating, floating down the ink-black river. And I know I must reach out and save us all somehow. I am terrified and rigid, looking for a branch, a tree, anything to grasp to save us from this black river that leads to that fall into the endless abyss of something that is not nothing which is also not us. It is the endless negation of us and I cry out for a reprieve and grab for one last story, one last memory that will be the branch that will save us. That will create a warm bubble of suspended time that will give us our protection in the memory of our mind. Then, just as our home is about to go over that black waterfall, I reach out and grasp the memory, a story.

We are all suddenly back at Kathie's grandmother's funeral and Marissa has just read her poem aloud beside the open casket of her great-grandmother. We have all followed the funeral procession to the church, and the coffin of Kathie's grandmother is raised high on a platform beside us. I can tell that Forrest is a little nervous about all that's going on. He both recognizes his great-grandmother and at the same time does not. He is acting a little jittery, as though he expects her body to pop up out of the coffin and all of a sudden come alive. Forrest is coping with all this in a rather delightful way. He is holding up what I suspect, for him, are two very powerful talismans, or transitional objects. They are two cards, and he is holding one in each hand, which he keeps moving in an almost choreographed ritualized way into different positions. First he holds the right hand high and the left hand low and then reverses them, not unlike the way the priest handles and swings his incense holder. I look to see what the cards are that he is holding and I see that one card is of a Dinobot, a creature that is half dinosaur and half robot, from a *Beast Wars* video. The other card, which makes for a bizarre and fantastic juxtaposition, is a postcard I bought him that past summer in Martha's Vineyard. The card must have turned up somewhere in the car on the way to the funeral, and now Forrest has reclaimed it and converted it into a transitional object. It's a cartoon caricature of a male and female couple trying to have a good time in the waters off the coast of Martha's Vineyard. There's a lighthouse in the distance. She is in a rowboat rowing, and he is right near the boat, floating and relaxing in an inner tube. Then right under him is a great white shark, jaws open, about to devour his lower extremities. The caption on the card reads, "Having a lovely time in Martha's Vineyard."

As Forrest waves and manipulates these two cards, the priest speaks over a microphone on the altar:

> *I implore you do not grieve and mourn for*
> *Ann today but rejoice and celebrate.*

And I see, to my delight, something I've not noticed before. I'm surprised that I've not noticed that the two cartoon caricatures in the postcard Forrest is holding are our President and his wife. Hillary is in the rowboat, and Bill is relaxing in an inner tube. I am almost laughing aloud when Forrest turns to me and says, "Dad, I got to pee. I got to pee so bad, Dad."

I lean over and whisper to him, "Great. Let's get outta here."

In the back of the church, locked in the men's room, we both try to pee. But there's no escape. The funeral is being broadcast over speaker boxes on the wall of the men's room. And we hear, as we try to pee:

> From this land of shadows into the eternal
> kingdom of glorious light. Let this be a
> day of celebration and not of mourning.

Under this funeral ceremony, Forrest and I are having our ritual ceremony of who can finish peeing into the toilet first. He always wins, of course, because his bladder is so much smaller than mine. I always act like his winning is a surprise and like I really try to beat him.

We have played this game often before, but this time Forrest does something new and unexpected. He looks directly at my penis after he finishes peeing. He just looks at it as though he's never seen it before and says, "Wow, Dad, look at your penis." Then, before asking him what is wrong with it, I respond nervously, "Yes, it's fifty-six years old and it's really been around."

Then Forrest cries out, "Wow! Fifty-six years old and it's not even a person!"

I laugh, the way only Forrest can get me to laugh, and at the same time I am laughing, I feel overwhelmed by so much love for him. I feel more love than I can stand or let in. Then what almost overrides that love, like a banner flying high over that funeral men's room, is another old epitaph from the historic cemetery which read:

It's a fearful thing to love what death can touch.

At that moment, when I am just about to let the love I feel for Forrest into my heart, I have a vision of what hell could be for me. Dying by chance (a vein in my brain pops for no apparent reason, just pops), I see my body lying on the floor of that men's room and I feel some leftover part of me trying to make it to some great all-consuming union, like a sperm swimming toward an egg. Then it is stopped by the love I still feel for my son standing there below me. It's that earthly love I still feel for Forrest that keeps the part of me that needs to dissolve from dissolving. This spirit of mine can neither come nor go, but just lingers in the limbo of love. All that is left of me is this horrid, lingering awareness that knows there is no longer any solid configuration of me that can touch and hold my son. It is a true horror. It's the making of a haunted ghost. This awareness knows that it can never ever kiss, touch, or hug this sweet child again. I can see him waiting to be touched, to be held. That is what I think of now as a perfect vision of hell. Now, as I stand there beside Forrest, the vision of that vision causes me to reach down and pull him into me and hold him tight, and I am there holding my son Forrest as I think, "Oh Forrest, child-light of my life, even now as I hold you I can feel time stealing you away."

This reverie has taken me down closer to sleep. I am about to drop into the arms of death's second self when I hear the brilliant cry of Theo. I hear him crying in his crib in the guest room. Needing to hold him so badly, I leap from the bed to try to beat Kathie to the guest room. Then I slow down when I realize that Kathie is sleeping.

I go into the guest room and pick Theo up out of his crib. I feel the way his body weight and the pliable contour of this warm bundle of flesh fits to me and sticks. Oh Theo, my for-better-or-for-worse anchor to this earth.

I carry him in and lay him beside Kathie, who is now awake. Theo bellies up to the milk bar and begins to tank up. He's lying between Kathie and me and he's kicking me while he sucks and I am going to sleep.

I am going to sleep being kicked by my son.